ONCE UPON A GARAGE SALE...

From Fairy Tale to Reality:

How to Make More Money, Get Rid of More Stuff, and Otherwise Succeed at Your Garage Sale

Lisa Rogovin Payne

First Edition, 1997

❖clover creations❖
Overland Park, Kansas

ONCE UPON A GARAGE SALE...

From Fairy Tale to Reality: How to Make More Money, Get Rid of More Stuff, and Otherwise Succeed at Your Garage Sale

by Lisa Rogovin Payne

Published by clover creations
P.O. Box 26422
Shawnee Mission, KS 66225-6422 U.S.A.

Copyright 1997
by Lisa Rogovin Payne
First Printing 1997
Printed in the United States of America
ISBN 0-9657137-2-5
Library of Congress Number 97-066241

Library of Congress Cataloging-in-Publication Data
(Prepared by Michael Readinger, Librarian)
Payne, Lisa Rogovin
       Once Upon A Garage Sale...From Fairy Tale to Reality: How to Make More Money, Get Rid of More Stuff, and Otherwise Succeed at Your Garage Sale / by Lisa Rogovin Payne.
       p. cm.
       ISBN 0-9657137-2-5
       1. Garage Sales   I. Title.
       HF5482.3.P38 1997
       658.8'7—dc21   97-066241
                                    CIP

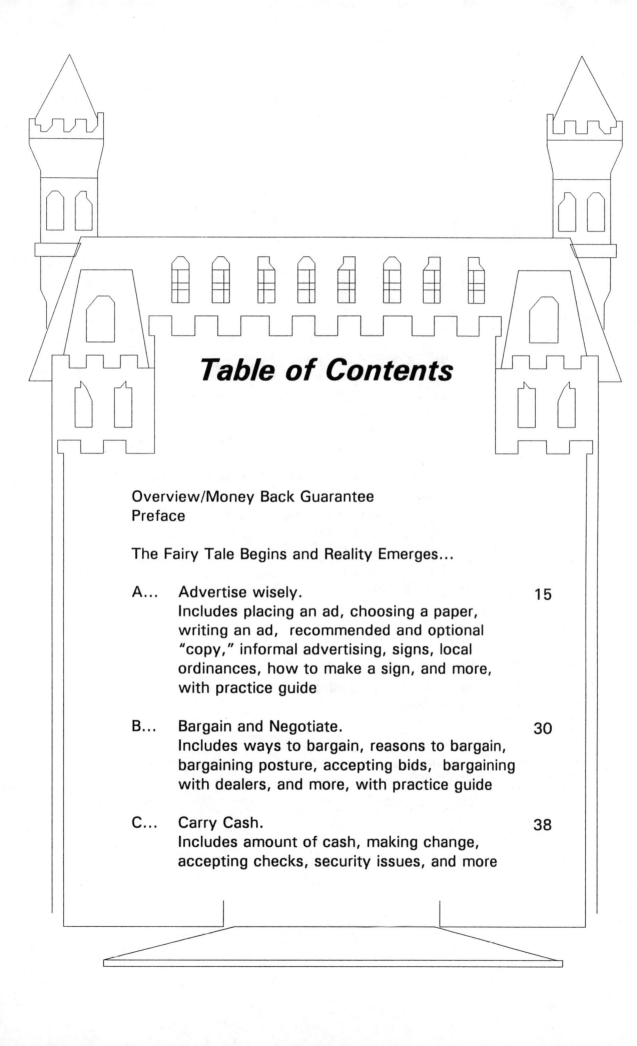

Table of Contents

Overview/Money Back Guarantee
Preface

The Fairy Tale Begins and Reality Emerges...

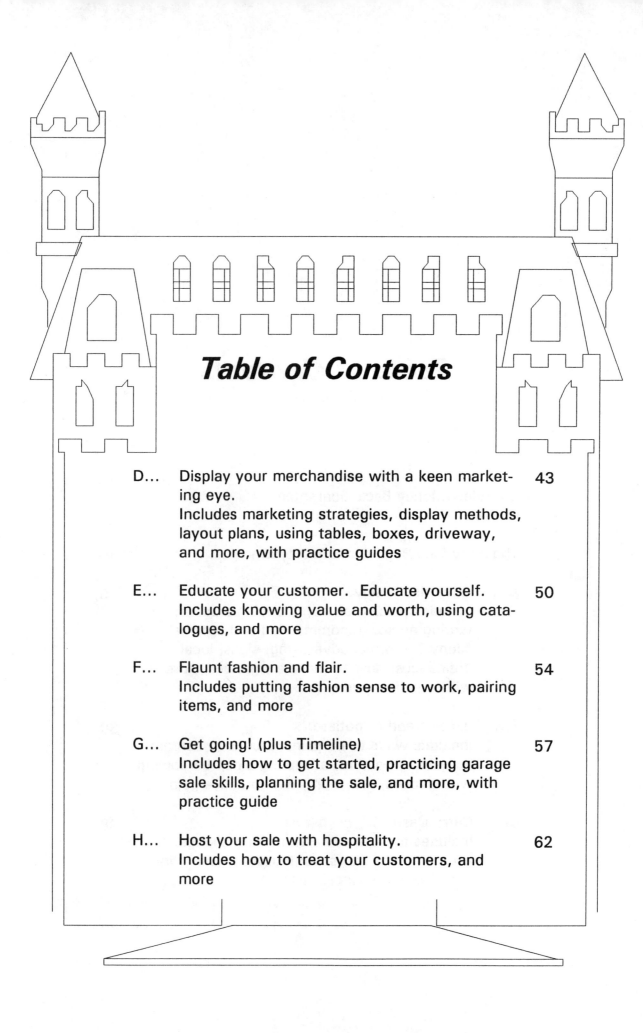

Table of Contents

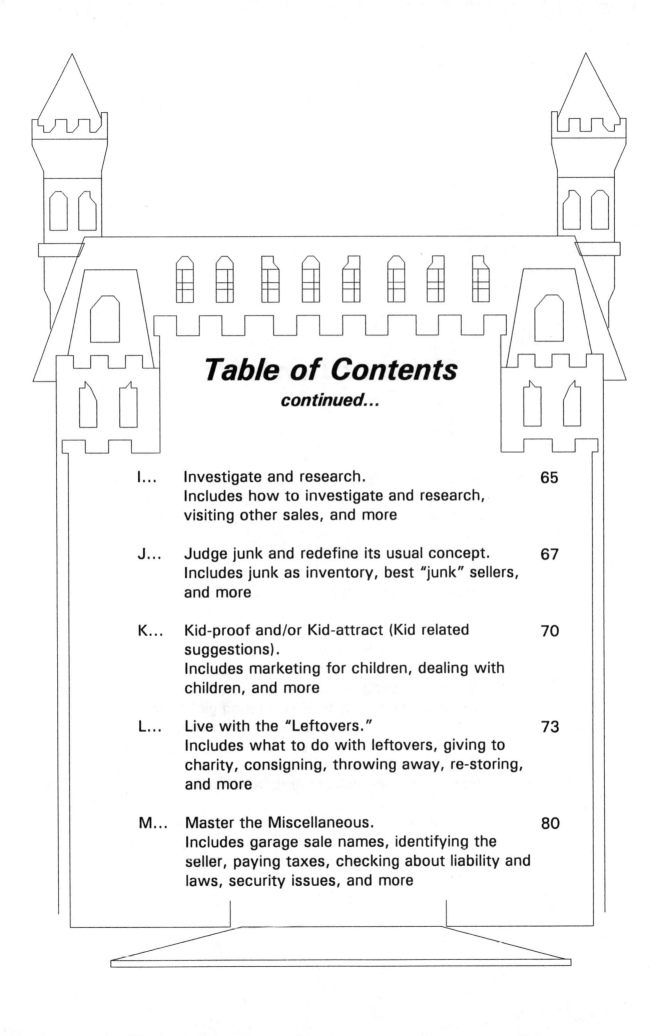

Table of Contents
continued...

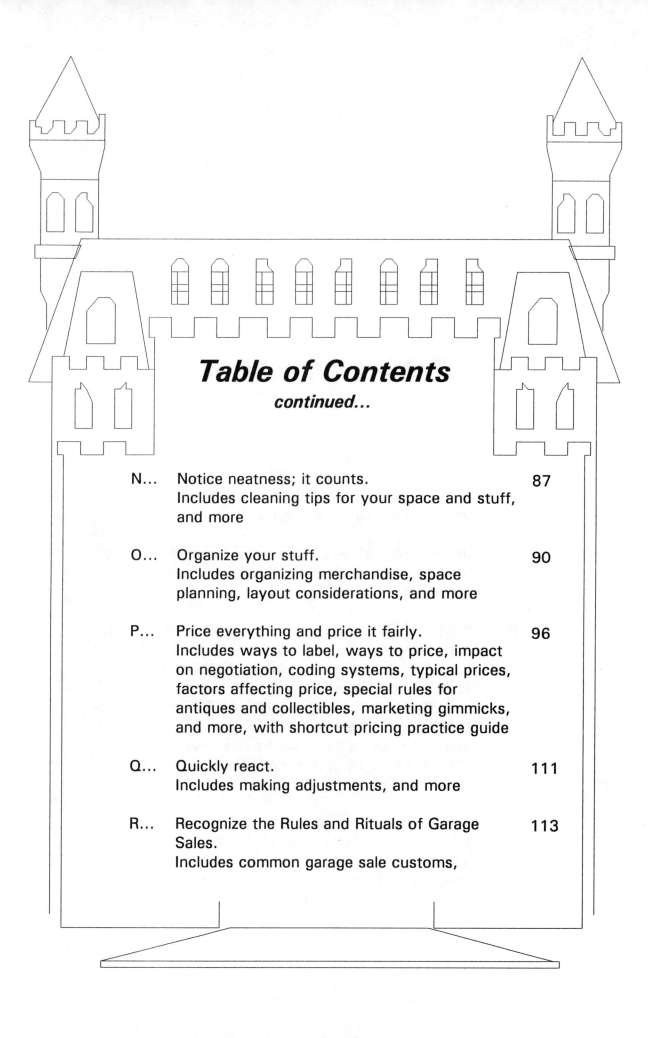

Table of Contents

continued...

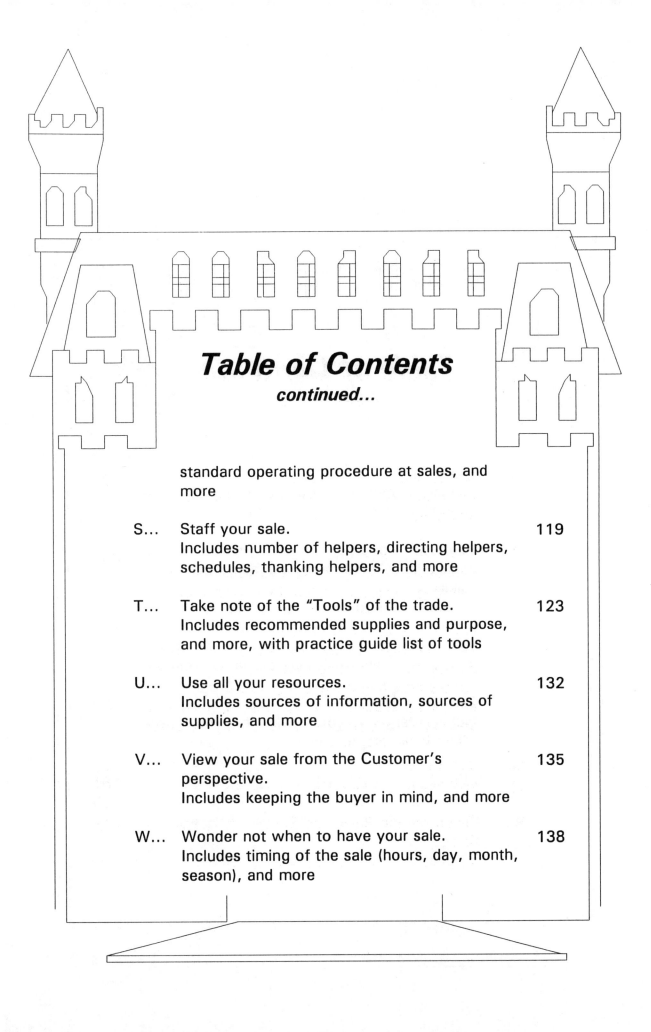

Table of Contents

continued...

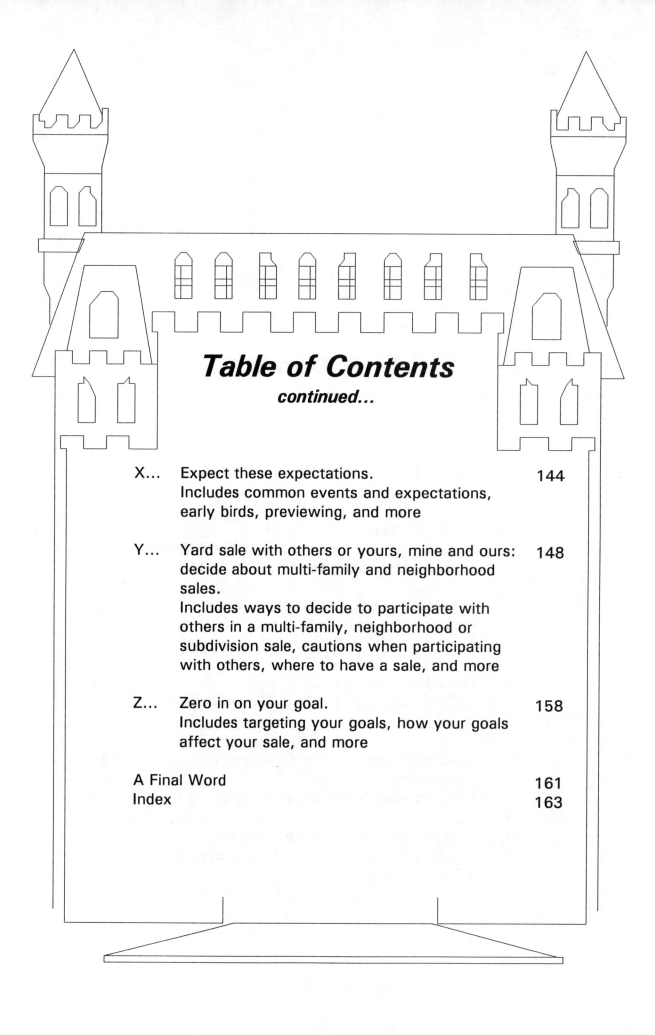

Table of Contents

continued...

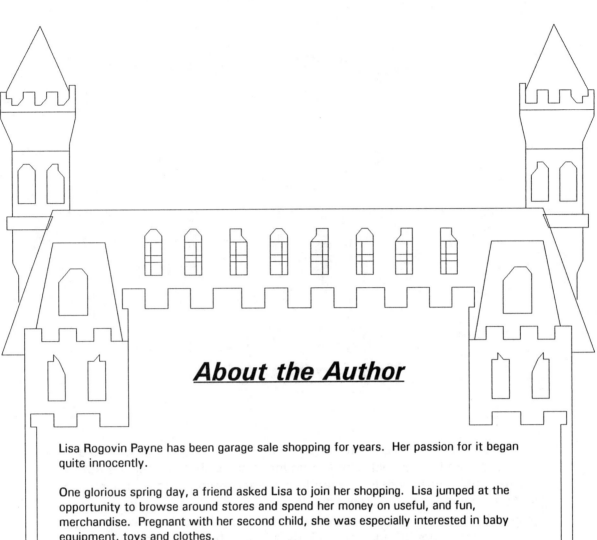

About the Author

Lisa Rogovin Payne has been garage sale shopping for years. Her passion for it began quite innocently.

One glorious spring day, a friend asked Lisa to join her shopping. Lisa jumped at the opportunity to browse around stores and spend her money on useful, and fun, merchandise. Pregnant with her second child, she was especially interested in baby equipment, toys and clothes.

On the way to the mall, the two friends noticed a series of pink, neon signs. Lisa paid little attention to the banners, but her friend, Alice, remembered fondly her garage sale days in Iowa and began talking about them out loud to Lisa. The two looked at each other, shrugged a "what the heck" kind of shrug, and made a bee-line for the advertised garage sale.

What started as a casual weekend diversion for a working mom steadily developed. The thrill of finding a terrific something at a fabulous price was exciting, to say the least. As Lisa spent less on the things she needed (kids' clothes, toys, books, and more), her interest in the sport of the garage sale grew. She was transformed from weekend garage sale warrior to a four-time a week garage sale guru.

With this much practice, and a questioning, analytical mind (comes from all those years as a lawyer), Lisa learned what it takes to make a garage sale successful. She decided to combine her love of the garage sale with her love of writing. The result is "Once Upon a Garage Sale...," a unique, comprehensive work about garage sales, just for sellers.

When not searching for the next garage sale bargain, Lisa can be found giving seminars about garage sales, consulting about garage sales, or enjoying and raising her two children with her husband of over fifteen years (not necessarily in that order!).

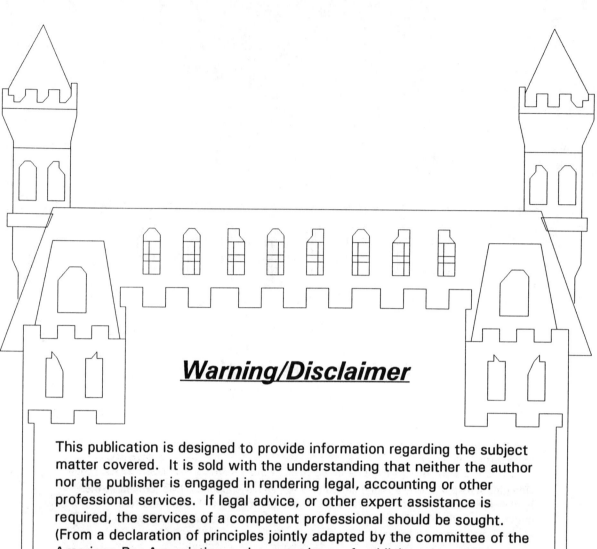

<u>*Warning/Disclaimer*</u>

This publication is designed to provide information regarding the subject matter covered. It is sold with the understanding that neither the author nor the publisher is engaged in rendering legal, accounting or other professional services. If legal advice, or other expert assistance is required, the services of a competent professional should be sought. (From a declaration of principles jointly adapted by the committee of the American Bar Association and a committee of publishers.)

Every effort has been made to make this book as complete and accurate as possible. However, there may be mistakes, both typographical and in content. The text should be used as a general guide, with information on the subject matter only up to the printing date.

The purpose of this book is to educate and entertain. Neither the author nor the publisher shall have liability or responsibility to any individual person or entity for any loss or damage which may be caused or alleged to be caused directly or indirectly from or by information contained within this book.

If you do not wish to be bound by the above, you may return this book to the publisher for a full refund.

Acknowledgments

A public "thank you" needs to be said to the many people who have played a role in the development of this book. There were encouragers; creative geniuses; constructive critics; resourceful allies; garage sale companions and devotees; and true friends. They know who they are, and you should too. A special "thank you" to (in alphabetical order): Valerie Baker, Judy Bryant, Claudette DeMuth, Peggy Elson, Sylvia Faulkes, Patti Friedman, Kathy Gregory, Kara Hakim, George and Vicki Hanley, Karen Harrell, Cherlyn Jakubowski, Marci Kellner, Jan Knese, Terry McJilton, Linda Miller, Richard Miller, Lisa Moore, Glenda Motes, Mary O'Connell, Kris Petersen of BK Enterprises, Debby Ranson, Debbie Rau, Lisa Round, Paula Rubino, and Alice Von Seggern.

An ironically anonymous "thank you" needs to be said to those residents and homeowners of Johnson County, Kansas, who have held garage sales during the last several years. Unknowingly, they have taught me, and continue to teach me, the finer points of garage sales salesmanship.

Many "professionals" have contributed to the finished product now before you. Whether paid for services provided or not, each individual or firm went beyond the norm, providing excellent service and counsel. These include (in alphabetical order): Dena Byington, Daniel Key (CPA), Pam Pugh-Jones, Ann McJilton, Linda McLean (McLean Designs), Jo Devine and Michael H. Readinger of the Johnson County Library, Marsha Sinetar (Author), Greg Trester (Personal Touch, Inc.), Mary Wells, and Marcia Wieder (Author).

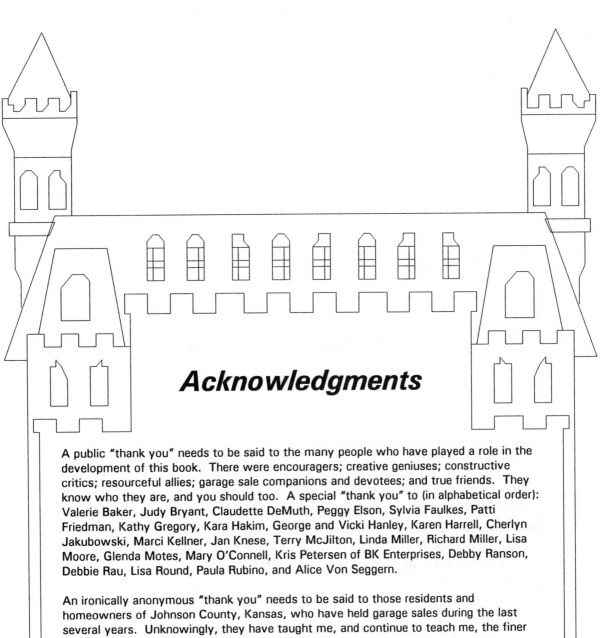

A different, but no less special "thank you" is also due my family: Roger, Jordan and Ross Payne; Aliene and George Payne; David and Patricia Rogovin; Marc and Mary Sheffield Rogovin; Tim and Wendy Rogovin Oskey; Leslie and Caty Payne; and Patricia Payne.

Overview and Money Back Guarantee

The Fairy Tale Begins and Reality Emerges

Once upon a time, there was a garage sale, an absolutely, positively marvelous garage sale. It was the best garage sale you can picture. The seller sold big and little items, old and new items, and everything in between. The buyer was very happy to buy the seller's treasures. Best of all, the seller made more money than the seller ever thought possible.

Sound like a fairy tale? It is not, or at least it does not have to be. It is and can be reality for you, as the seller at your garage sale, if you follow the advice in this book.

What do you have to lose? Nothing, plain and simple. If "Once Upon a Garage Sale..." does not show you how to make more money at your garage sale than you paid for this book, return your copy of the book with your receipt to the publisher's address for a full refund.

Preface

You are clearly on your way to garage sale success with the purchase of this book...

As with every venture, especially a money-making one, being knowledgeable and prepared will pay off. (Obviously, you have already recognized this. You are clearly on your way to garage sale success with the purchase of this book!)

> This Handbook has been set up to correspond with the letters of the alphabet. There is garage sale advice for every letter of the alphabet, providing readers with useful information in a fun format.

For fun and ease, this book has been set up to correspond to the letters of the alphabet.

Each of the letters of the "garage sale alphabet" provides invaluable hints, suggestions and ideas, forming a comprehensive how-to manual for you as a seller. Despite its thoroughness, however, this handbook is not exhaustive. By definition, it cannot be. It is meant to be a fluid, dynamic handbook, changing and developing with you, given your own experiences. It encourages your input and involvement.

You are encouraged to use this book as the base of a pyramid, the foundation of a building, or the four corners of a puzzle. When you choose to use the book this way, you will build on what you have learned and become even more successful, from hour to hour during your sale, from day to day of your sale and from your first garage sale to the next one.   Be creative.   Be resourceful. Expand.   Grow.

Have fun while making more money.

Most importantly, have fun, while making more money!

For Your Notes...

A is for...

Advertise Wisely.

Place an ad.

Begin by placing an ad in a local newspaper. The ad should appear in the classified section, preferably under the heading "Garage Sales." (There is an overview practice guide at the end of this chapter to help put all the information together.)

Select a local newspaper.

Choose a local newspaper which garage sale shoppers consider their "Bible." Usually that is not the local metropolitan daily. Because of advertising rates, and because there is no cost to residents, the bi-weekly paper tends to be your best bet.

Shopper type publications or "penny savers" may be a good advertising spot also.

How do you know in which paper to advertise? There are several options.

If you are unsure about which paper to advertise in, there are several simple ways to make this decision.

---

1. Ask anyone you know who has had a garage sale where they advertised and if they were satisfied with the result.

Ask friends about their sales.

2. Ask any friend or neighbors who attend sales what their source of information is for a particular sale.

3. Quickly review the number of entries in the "Garage Sales" column within several different newspapers. This should provide you with a sense of what the market place knows. If "The Times" newspaper lists 5 garage sales in your town and "The Bulletin" newspaper provides 25 entries, chances are readers (and would be customers) refer to "The Bulletin" newspaper. You should advertise within "The Bulletin" newspaper.

You may want to advertise in more than one paper.

You may want to place an ad in more than one newspaper. If your ad will be seen and acted on, it is generally well worth your money to place the ad. You are not limited to one ad only.

Plan on a three-line ad.

Avoid going overboard with your ad. A 3-line ad should be enough for most garage sales. (Ask the classified department what is the usual number of lines for a garage sale or pick up the paper yourself and take note.)

Arrange for your ad to appear on the day of the sale, and on the day before the sale.

Arrange for your ad to appear on the day(s) of your sale and at least one day before the first day of your sale as well.

Garage Sale

~

8 - 5 today
1234 Main St.
Anytown, USA

Advertise Wisely

Place your ad within the paper's deadlines.

Check with the media source (newspaper, bulletin, etc.) to find out their rates (how much does it cost to run an ad) and deadlines (when you have to place an ad). Make sure you place your ad within these timeframes and deadlines.

> **NOTE: It is often cheaper to have your ad appear for more than one day. Do not hesitate to ask the salesperson at the paper what is the cheapest way to run a garage sale ad.**

Always check your ad for accuracy.

Make sure that you check your ad for accuracy, as soon as it appears in the newspaper. Contact the paper immediately if there is an error. Ask the paper to correct the ad. You should do everything possible yourself to make the ad right, especially if the error is on a key item, such as your address. (This is another good reason to have your ad appear on the day before the sale.) For example, if the address is wrong and you cannot get it changed before your sale, go to the wrong address listed, and place a sign there to tell them where your sale really is being held.

List the "major" sale items in your ad. You want to draw people to your sale; tell your customers what they want to know about your stuff to make them come to your sale.

The "copy" (that is, the substance of your ad, what is said in print) should always list the major items of your sale. "Major" may relate

Advertise Wisely

17

to the most expensive items you have to sell or the most plentiful, the ones you have the most of at your sale. Generally, you should state a category of items, rather than a specific good (furniture versus chair; toys versus pogo stick). Make an exception to this rule if you have only one item of the category or if the particular item is extremely saleable (such as a roll-top desk or a battery-operated car/jeep).

The "copy" should also clearly, without fanfare or opinion, tell the selling point of the item. Remember that you want to draw people to your house or apartment: What do you need to tell them about your merchandise that will motivate them to come to the sale? Ask yourself that question and cut your response down to be manageable in print (that is, affordable) since you are paying for your ad by the character, letter, word or line.

Abbreviate where possible in your ad.

Abbreviate when possible in your ad. Ask the sales person at the newspaper to help you with abbreviations. They will generally suggest some, given their experience and skills.

NOTE: Many times manufacturer's names are stated in an ad. These are often abbreviated. Examples: Fisher Price as FP, Liz Claiborne as Liz, etc.

Advertise Wisely

Some items in your ad are a must: the days, date, time, and place.

There are certain essentials in ad "copy."

State the day(s) and dates of the sale with the hours of the sale (such as Wed-Sat, 5/15 to 5/18, 8-2), and an address or general location (such as Main and Oak --follow signs).

> **Recently, a great, but fatally flawed ad appeared in the newspaper; it began, "Don't miss this one..." and included a mouthwatering list of items available at the sale. It told when the sale would be held, but left out the location. There was no specific or general street address or location given for the sale. Pretty hard to "not miss the sale" if you don't know where it is!**

There are some items which are optional in your ad.

There are some items which are optional in your ad. You decide. (Our recommendations are stated.)

1. Do not list your telephone number. You will only be bombarded with calls before, during and after your sale. These calls most likely will not help your sale, and probably will hurt it. You may also be setting yourself up for security scams by giving your phone number.

Give directions to your sale.

2. If your house is difficult to find or is not on a main street, consider giving general directions in the ad. This is really cost advantageous in the long run; while you are paying for extra words in the ad, you are probably bringing people to the sale who otherwise would not know where the sale is.

Advertise Wisely

State your directions simply, such as Prairie La., 2 blocks east of Hardy, bw. Lewis and Green Streets.

State any rules.

3. If you feel strongly about garage sale protocol (see Chapter "R," Recognized Rules & Rituals), you may want to state certain garage sale rules. Ex: no early birds. Most people ignore this anyway, so unless you have a large budget, don't bother with these words.

Are you moving?

4. If you are moving, or having an estate sale, state this in your ad. People presume that you would rather sell an item at a bargain to the shopper, than pay to move it. (Chances are, they are right!)

Rain or shine?

5. If you will have your sale even if it is raining, you may wish to say this in your ad. (The usual language set forth is "Rain or Shine.")

Why pay for these words? Not everyone will have their sale if it is raining. A lot of shoppers will be out and about regardless of the weather and they may make a bee-line for your sale knowing in advance that it will be held. Shoppers are understandably frustrated if they drive to a garage sale and the garage door is shut, just because of a little rain! If you are unsure of the regional practice, check it out on a rainy Saturday or ask around in the sunshine.

NOTE: If your area of the country typically has sales "rain or shine," do not bother stating this in your ad.

Ads are in order in the newspaper, alphabetically or otherwise.

All ads are arranged in some way. It may be alphabetical, by address, by geographic location or by first come, first served. Many ads are arranged in the newspaper alphabetically. If that is the way your paper arranges its ads, consider starting your copy with a word from the beginning of the alphabet, rather than the end. Since readers may lose interest after the 25th entry in the "garage sale" column, it is generally advantageous to start your ad with the word, "ANTIQUES," rather than the words, "YARD sale, antiques."

Most garage sale ads are arranged in alphabetical order...

If your newspaper doesn't arrange alphabetically, try to find out, or figure out, how the ads are arranged by the paper. Your object is to get your ad to the top of the column, and you can get there, to the top, with a minimum of effort, by slightly changing your ad.

> **Again, ask the sales representative "how can I get my ad to be the first or second one?" Follow that advice if at all possible.**

Be creative with your ad.

Try to be creative with your ad. If you are so inclined or so talented, be witty, cute and clever with your words. Certain words create interest, almost by definition. These include: large, big, huge, multi-family (or MF), bargains, antiques, consignment-quality, name brands, designer, free, junque, new, neighborhood/subdivision sale, moving, estate sale, and retiring. Numbers also attract a lot of interest, such as 20-year accumulation, and 100+ dresses.

Use interesting words and numbers.

You can learn from other peoples' sales.

❖ Recognize, once again, that you can learn from others before you. Review some ads for sales in the paper and see what kinds of things are set forth routinely (such as garage sale rules) and what words attract you. Make the most of your own observations.

Advertise informally.

Informally advertise as well. Use word of mouth, telling anyone/ everyone you can think of that you are having a sale. After you get the necessary permission, post notices at or on grocery store bulletin boards, employee lunchrooms at your

> Did you hear about Ann's sale?

Advertise Wisely

place of work, and the like.

❖ You may want to invite your friends or neighbors to your house the night or day before the sale for a "by invitation only" showing of your sale.

Use signs as a kind of "ad."

Use yard and directional signs as a form of advertisement. Signs should be on either hot pink/fuchsia, bright yellow, orange or chartreuse green heavy paper (poster board generally works) with black permanent marker writing. The bright colors are suggested to attract the attention of the passerby, who did not otherwise know about your sale, or to direct the driver who has seen your ad and is looking for your sale.

Make sure your signs are legible. Use bright colors.

Give your signs the same look.

You may want to consider giving your signs all the same look or design, for easy recognition and identification. Examples: all your signs may be hot pink with purple writing, or have balloons or crepe paper as a border, or display a certain, non-copyrighted cartoon character (how about a garage sale prince or princess?) which you might enlarge on a copier and glue and color alike from sign to sign.

Protect signs against the weather.

Consider wrapping your signs in plastic wrap to protect against rain.

It is critical that any writing on the sign be

Make sure your signs are legible and simple.

legible. That means the writing must be neat, clear and large enough to be read at 30 mph.

Your sign should state your address (either 200 Main Street) or a general location (Main and Second Street) or simply give directional arrows.

❖   While directional signs are easy to follow, they might direct your buyer to another sale or may be taken by a less hard-working seller for their future sale.

Make sure your signs point to your house.

Your signs should be simple, too. It is hard to read about the details of your sale on a sign while traveling in traffic.

Put date and time on your signs.

It is helpful to put the day and time of your sale on the sign. People do not appreciate it when they follow a sign and find out that the signs related to a sale held the weekend before.

Be ready to put up your signs.

The ultimate, overprepared garage sale seller recognizes that it is not always as easy as it may seem to put up a sign. Your list of possible supplies are: Regular carpenter's claw hammer, heavier sledge hammer, nails, heavy duty staple gun (with staples), wooden stakes (2 x 4 posts), masking tape, duct tape, wire, string, plastic wrap, and bricks.

❖   A good dimension for a sign is 18 inches by 24 inches.

Place your signs at as many nearby intersections as you can, depending on where

Advertise Wisely

Place signs everywhere.

you live. At a minimum, there should be a sign on your street and at every entry to your street or subdivision.

Check local ordinances.

Do not put a sign on a stop sign or other traffic device. Make sure that there are no laws, ordinances or rules preventing you from placing a sign at a particular location. Also, there is generally a restriction, forbidding you from putting a sign on a utility pole. Don't risk committing a trespass on someone else's property, especially, a potentially strong opponent like the local power company.

Use wooden stakes for your signs.

Your sign can be placed on a wooden pole, or other kind of pole or stake and hammered into the ground. You can also put your signs on a box or boxes with something heavy inside to hold them down.

> **Warning: Check your signs during the day(s) of your sale to make sure they are still in place and visible.**

Be a good neighbor, especially about signs.

Make sure you ask your neighbors if you may place a sign on their property.

Be a good neighbor yourself and pick up your signs after your garage sale is done.

Advertise Wisely

For Your Notes...

Advertise Wisely

Analysis and Criticism
of Advertisements *

Text of Ad	Analysis and Criticism positive and negative comments about the ad
"Garage Sale and salesman's samples. Sat only 8-5. 1111 Glenwood."	Doesn't tell shopper what is for sale. Is the salesman selling tools or women's clothes? What is the discount? How do you know if it is a good deal without additional information?
"Three family, lots of items, Weds-Sat 8-5, 2222 W 93rd St."	Doesn't tell the shopper what is for sale, although suggests there is a lot. Might want to quantify "a lot." Could have abbreviated more, ex., three as 3. Good to refer to multi-family. No catch phrase or hook.
"Back to school clothes sale, dishwasher, baseball cards, super misc. Thurs-Fri 8-4, Sat 8-2, 3333 Twilight La."	Good opening phrase, but does not complete the thought. What size clothes, for preschool or college? Good listing of hours. Probably need directions to this location.
"4444 Halsey, Misc. HH, sofa, some clothing. Fri-Sat 8-4."	No catch phrase. Abbreviation may not be readily known - does HH stand for household? What size clothing? Adult or kids?
"Big stuff, kid's stuff, many families selling great stuff. Wed 5-7 p.m., Thurs 9-4, Fri 9-2. 5555 129th Terr. (Watch for signs at 129th & Mission)"	Great opening-cute and well positioned, but it needs to give you a greater flavor of what is at the sale. Good listing of hours and directions.
"Remodeling sale - oven, liv rm furn, bunk beds, area rugs, lamps, fplc door, drapes, blinds, linens, toys plus lots misc. 6666 Marty Aug. 3-6."	Good opening and good listing of merchandise. Left out hours of the sale.
"Like new designer clothes: Polo, Nautica, Gap, Gymboree, boy's, girl's, men's ladies, shoes, household items, much misc. 7777 W. 114th Wed-Sat."	Good reference to namebrands or manufacturers. No hours listed.
"Jefferson, 8888-Antiques, lawn eqpt, dishes, trunk, books, records, clothes. You name it, we've got it! 8-5 Wed., Thurs., Fri., Sat."	Awkward placement of info-hook should go first. Why not say Wed-Sat?

* All ads are real and have actually appeared in the local Kansas City papers. The only changes made were to the street addresses. Any phone numbers were eliminated.

Advertise Wisely

Practice Guide

Putting It All Together: How to Write a Dynamite Ad

In order to write a dynamite ad, there are some things to consider:

What about your sale will create interest and attract shoppers to it? You may want to begin with a "sound bite" or "hook," a catchy phrase, usually talking about reasons for your sale and/or the quality and quantity of your stuff for sale. Some good examples of this technique are:

Awesome Multi-family sale
Cramped for space, must sell
Priced to sell
Annual fund-raiser for scouts
Bargain hunters come early
All priced to sell

What descriptive words best describe ***your*** sale?

____

____

What are your most expensive items for sale? What items do you have the most of to sell? What items do you have that are the most popular or are best sellers? Some examples of this are:

Designer wm. clothes, size 4-12, incl. Liz, Jones NY, Picone
Avon bottles, depression glass, collectibles, hshld misc.
Baby equip and furn, namebrand clothes 0-4t
Furniture, exercise eqpt, books, adult clothes

What do **you** have that others may be particularly interested in buying?

____

____

As you prepare to write your ad, keep in mind that there are some mandatory and optional points to include in your ad.

The <u>mandatory</u> facts about the sale that need to be included in your ad are:

When is your sale? (Time and Date)

Where is your sale? (Street Address and Location, if necessary)

What is for sale? What are your major items?

There are some **optional** facts that may make your ad more enticing to potential shoppers:

State rules that you want to abide by. ("No Early Birds" or "Cash Only")

Why are you having the sale? (Are you moving? Retiring? Cleaning house? Need cash fast? Having an annual event?)

Who is having the sale? (Is it a neighborhood sale? A multi-family sale? A pack-rat? A sorority? Etc.)

You are now ready to draft your ad. Use your answers to the questions above to create an interesting and catchy ad. To create interest and attract shoppers to your sale, you may want to begin with a "sound bite" or "hook, " usually talking about reasons for the sale. Next, list the major items you have in your sale. Do not be too specific, keeping to general catagories of stuff. State the facts (when and where your sale will be held - do not give your phone number). State any other pertinent details.

_____

_____

_____

_____

Edit and review your draft. Did you use abbreviations as much as possible (on every word, or every other word, and still have the ad make sense)? Can the words be cuter? Funnier? More catchy? Stand out more? Did you start with a letter from the beginning of the alphabet (if that's the way your local newspaper arranges its ads)? A? B? C? D? E? Did you make every word count? Does every word show or help to show why a garage sale shopper should come to your sale first? Would you? Count the number of words. Is it too short or long?

Try again!

_____

_____

_____

Advertise Wisely

B is for...

Bargain and negotiate.

For most shoppers, the fun of garage sale shopping is the bargain.

For many, if not most, garage sale shoppers, the fun, the "kick," of garage sale shopping is in the bargain, the deal and its making.

Shoppers expect, and truly appreciate, the opportunity to dicker over a particular price. If you refuse to negotiate, you are simply upsetting the natural balance and order of things, as far as a garage sale shopper is concerned.

Negotiation does not need to be intimidating.

It is not necessary to get intimidated by the thought of, and process involved in, negotiating. Make the potential buyer do the work of negotiating, at least the lion's share of it.

Since your labeled or stickered price is the first "offer," let the shopper counter that offer. He/she may say, for example, "Will you take less for this item?" You should respond "Probably, what do you have in mind? "or "Could be, what will you pay me for it?" The dickering usually progresses with ease from this point. (A practice guide or worksheet is

Bargain and Negotiate

attached at the end of this chapter. It lists common sayings and responses.)

Pricing can definitely affect negotiations.

NOTE: It is often curious just how much your pricing can affect negotiating. Let us say that you are trying to sell a rocking chair. You have tagged it $25.00 Chances are that you will receive an offer somewhere between $15.00 and $20.00. If you had not priced the item, you could (and probably would) get an offer for as little as $5.00. It is harder to negotiate when you are $20.00 apart than when you are $10.00 or $5.00 off.

Let the shopper begin bargaining.

It is important to let the shopper begin the bargaining process. Do not mark down your own price voluntarily, just because the shopper asked you to. Wait first to get some input from the shopper. If you do, chances are that you will sell your item for less than the buyer is willing to pay. This is common at a sale.

Example: Let us say you have a set of books for sale. They are priced at $1.00/book and there are 50 of them. Someone asks you if you will sell them cheaper if he/she buys all of the books. You say "okay" and volunteer that $25.00 is acceptable. Although you did not know it, the buyer was willing to pay as much as $45.00 for the books. You would have lost $20.00 for no reason at all.

Negotiate for one or two rounds.

One round of negotiation is usually the norm. Two is generally the maximum. Beyond that, at the standard garage sale, it is true "nickel diming." (Example: The shopper says "will you take $5.00?" "No, I'll take $10.00," you answer. The shopper continues, "what about

$7.50?" You should generally accept or go back to your $10.00 counter. It doesn't need to go back and forth much more than this.)

You can take bids on items, but be careful.

Remember that you can decide to take bids on an item. If the shopper and you cannot agree on the price of an item, encourage the shopper to leave his/her name and telephone number. Then you can call the shopper back in the event that you do not get your asking price. But, be careful. It is actually quite rare for a seller to call back.

The typical seller is likely to be worn down by the end of the sale, and, therefore, may sell the item to another bidder (one with even a less favorable price- after all that buyer is at the sale with the cash right then and there). Or, even if the typical seller stuck to his/her price, the chance that the seller kept that little piece of paper with the buyer's name, number and offer on it is not great, and even less likely that the typical seller will have found that paper after the sale itself.

Allow room for negotiatiation.

Build negotiation into your asking price in the first place. If for example, you want to get $15.00 for an item, consider pricing it at $17.50 or $20.00. If you expect to earn $1.00 for your merchandise, price it at $1.25 or $1.50.

❖   Note the interesting added benefit to this

strategy. Many people will pay the asking price (especially occasional garage sale shoppers) without any negotiation or question. Your cushion is just that, a cushion, and the cushion monetarily allows you to take the risk, the risk of a reduced amount on another item, for the sake of the garage sale game.

Non-negotiation may ruin a sale.

People, in general, resist stubborness and firmness. It is human nature for a customer to be turned off by a seller who is headstrong and inflexible about a price. There is no reason to take that approach, especially if you want to make money at your garage sale. Reducing your price by as little as fifty cents is much better than not reducing at all.

Keep negotiating in perspective.

Try to keep negotiating in perspective. To do this, ask yourself several questions. (This is a non-exhaustive list; it is aimed at helping you identify your goals and gain your own, workable, garage sale outlook and attitude.)

❖ Do you want to make the sale worth your while?

❖ Do you want to re-pack and store the item?

Bargain and Negotiate

What is the money difference really worth to you?

❖ What can you buy with the money at issue? What can you buy with the dollar difference between what you are willing to sell the item for and the buyer wants to pay? (Is that amount more or less than the cost of lunch at a fast food restaurant?)

❖ Can you consign the item if it does not sell at your sale? Will you?

❖ Is it the beginning of your sale or the end?

Are you bargaining with a "dealer?"

Most bargaining tactics do not apply to dealers, those people who make their living by going to garage sales and re-selling what they buy at the sale for a sizable profit. Pay attention and try to determine whether you are dealing with such a professional.

There are ways to tell if you are dealing with a "dealer."

How do you know? Often they tell. Other times, they are pretty obvious. They may come around in large trucks, with writing on the vehicle announcing their "flea market dealership" or "consignment" store. They tend to be abrupt, and very focused; they do not waste time looking for a lot of different things, but rather head for a certain kind of item (antiques, jewelry, furniture, kids' clothes). They carry a lot of cash. They "volume buy," that is, they buy a lot, way more than an average shopper would. (For example, they are interested in buying all of your books, all of your designer clothes, etc.)

Bargain and Negotiate

Do you care if you are bargaining with a "dealer?"

Why do you care? Dealers are very revealing. If a dealer is intererested in an item, the dealer has predetermined that the item is worth more, perhaps way more, than you have priced the item. That means you are likely to sell it, even if you do not sell it to the dealer on the dealer's terms. Dealers generally are good and stubborn negotiators. They know what they can pay you because they have calculated what they will re-sell the item for later. The lower they buy the item for from you, the greater their profit. They have a huge incentive to get you to lower the price.

Dealers can give you an idea of what is valuable and what is not...

There is a "dealer" solution.

Solution: You can afford to be more firm and hard-nosed on your price with a dealer. Encourage the dealer to come back at the end of the sale if he or she does not want to pay your price now. And, when other, non-dealer shoppers look at the item, you may even tell that shopper that you expect the dealer to come back for the item, meaning that the dealer expects to sell it for a least double the price, and suggest that you would much rather sell it to the non-dealer shopper.

Negotiation should be a positive experience for both buyer and seller.

Negotiation should always be win-win for both parties. The seller and the buyer must both feel as if they "won," that each got what they wanted. Bottom line: If you do not negotiate, you will hurt your bottom line, your profit.

Bottom line - negotiate!

Bargain and Negotiate

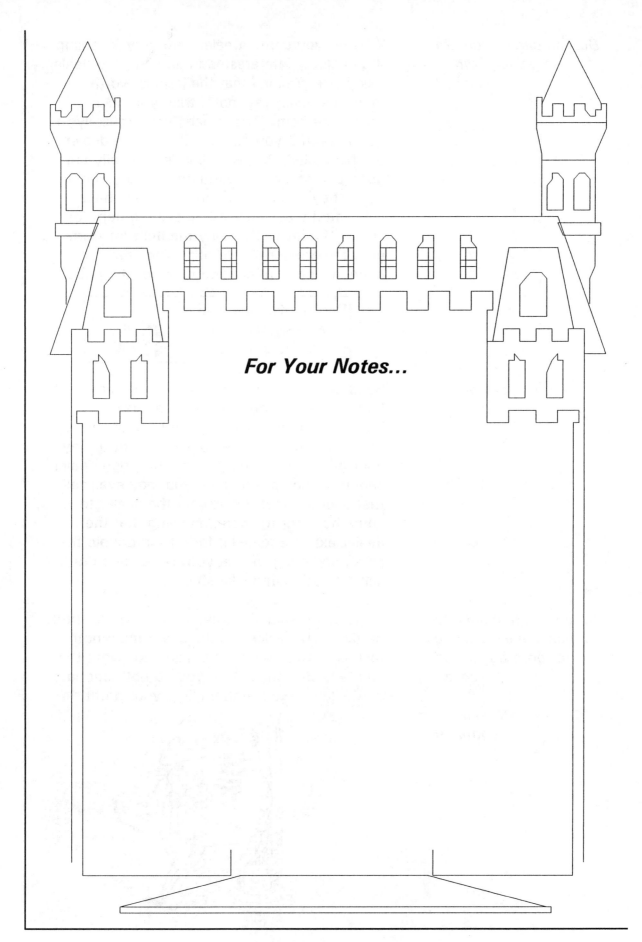

For Your Notes...

Bargain and Negotiate

Bargaining Practice Tips

If the shopper says:	You, as seller, say:
"Will you take less for this item?"	"Probably, what do you have in mind?" or "Could be, what will you pay me for it?"
"Are you firm on this price?"	"Not necessarily. What do you have in mind?" or "On that item, I am, but on most everything else, I am willing to negotiate." (If that is true.)
"Are your prices negotiable?"	"Mostly, especially on the higher priced items or if you buy a lot of stuff."
"Do you give volume discounts?"	"Generally, yes. The more stuff you buy, the more likely I am to negotiate on a total price."
On a $20.00 item, "Will you take $10.00 for this?"	"No, but I'll take $17.50/$15.00" (or whatever amount you are willing to take.) If the amount offered is way off your price, stay high, but come down; if it's on target, accept the offer.
On a $50.00 item, "Will you take $15.00 for this?"	"No at this point in the sale (it has just started) but if you want to leave your name and phone number, I'll consider your $15.00 bid after the sale is over." or "Not at this point; you may want to come back on Saturday when the sale is winding down," or "No, I'll go down to $45.00 only."

I'll give you 10.25 for that...

Bargain and Negotiate

C is for...

Carry cash.

Begin with about $70.00 in cash.

The cash you should have on hand at the beginning of your sale is $70.00 ("starter funds"). It is broken down as follows:

$16.00	in singles	(16 x $1.00)
$20.00	in five dollar bills	(4 x $5.00)
$30.00	in ten dollar bills	(3 x $10.00)
$ 3.00	in quarters	(12 x $ .25)
$ .50	in dimes	(5 x $ .10)
$ .50	in nickles	(10 x $ .05)
$70.00	Total	$70.00

Double the amount of cash on hand (starter funds) for a large sale (one where you reasonably expect to make $500.00 or more).

It is often confusing making change.

There is often confusion in the process of making change. There are several options in this regard.

Use your pockets.

1. Take and distribute your "starter funds" into your pockets. (You will need to wear clothing with front and rear pockets.) Put singles in your right front pocket, fives and tens in your left front pocket, twenty dollar bills in your back right pocket and change in your waist pouch. This system separates the money without having to sort through it as you are making change.

Carry Cash

Use a fanny pack.

2. Put all money received from the sale and all of your starter funds in a "fanny pack" (waist pouch). The starter funds can be paper clipped by type of bill ($1, $5, $10, $20) to keep the money sorted.

3. Use the fanny pack for the money you receive from your sale only and use your pockets for your original starter funds only. In other words, make change with the starter funds. Don't add to it otherwise.

4. Make up a note or a receipt showing how much money you put in as starter funds. Then keep all your money together in a fanny pack. Keep the bigger bills in the back and ones and fives in front.

Use a cash box or other secure place for your money.

5. Use a cash box (purchased at an office supply store, or perhaps available for free from your own bank), or a makeshift substitute such as a toolbox or shoe box, to separate your money. There may be a serious disadvantage to this system however, at least for the solo garage sale seller. With this system, you are tied to the cash machine; you cannot leave your post and help your customers (encourage sales, answer questions, keep an eye on your

Carry Cash

merchandise, bargain and negotiate(!), etc.) without unfortunately risking that the cash will be taken. The solution would be to have one helper with nothing to do but handle the money.

SCAM ALERT...Rumor has it that there are unscrupulous individuals around, posing as shoppers. They pick out an inexpensive item (costing $1.00 or less) and offer to pay for it with a larger bill, such as a ten. They then insist that they gave you a twenty. Some sellers, in an effort to avoid this unlikely event, put all twenty dollar bills inside immediately upon receipt. (You rarely need to make change with a twenty.) There is another possible way to avoid this scam. When making change for a customer, lay the bill that they gave you on your posterboard, notebook or table, or hold it in one hand, until you count the change back to them. This assures you that the change is correct and may well avoid any confusion.

Don't count cash where customers can see it.

Empty your pockets, waist pouch, or other money holder inside your house or apartment, out of view. Do the emptying at a natural break, when there is little traffic at your sale (even great sales have an occasional lull) or when nature calls. It is not recommended that you take the time to count your proceeds until the sale is completely over.

A garage sale is a cash and carry transaction.

A garage sale is generally a cash and carry transaction. Most shoppers know and respect this. By the same token, most shoppers expect to spend $15.00 to $20.00 at a particular sale or perhaps even on a given day.

You may be asked to accept a check.

It is not unusual therefore to be asked by a shopper if you will accept a check.

Carry Cash

When deciding to accept a check, take certain precautions.

The decision to accept checks is a personal one, tied to your level of comfort and risk-like or dislike. Experience indicates that garage sale shoppers are good for the money, as written on a check, a negotiable instrument. In fact, experience suggests that shoppers view checks more as credit than cash. Customers are more likely and more eager to buy (by volume and dollar amount) if they do not have to pay with cold, hard green cash.

If you decide not to accept a check, give the customer other options to buy anyhow.

If you still are reluctant to accept checks, a rule of thumb might allow a shopper to write a check if the total of purchases is more than a certain amount (such as $20.00). Other check guidelines require that the check is drawn on a local bank (not an out-of-town one) and that the check is not a two or more party instrument (it is written by your shopper and not just endorsed by him/her). It is perfectly reasonable for you to see the buyer's driver's license and to write its number on the check; it is equally proper for you to get the buyer's telephone number and/or social security number.

Carry Cash

If you decide not to accept a check, give other alternatives to accepting a check:

1. Offer to hold the item for a certain length of time while the shopper gets cash.

2. Ask for some cash and agree to accept the balance in a check.

Refrain from broadcasting your check writing policy, no matter what it is.

It is not advisable to broadcast your check writing policy, no matter what it is. To do so, invites hassles.

For Your Notes...

Carry Cash

D is for...

Display your merchandise with a keen marketing eye.

Do whatever is necessary to create a place where buyers want to buy.

Showcase your merchandise, your stuff, to increase its sales potential. In other words, market your stuff. Do whatever is necessary (considering what you have to sell) to create an organized, user friendly, buying environment. Do whatever you can to make a shopper want to come to your sale, buy tons of stuff at your sale and make paying easy and painless.

Interest passersby.

You want to lure passersby in to your sale; you want to keep current shoppers interested (the more they look at, the more they are likely to buy) and you want all lookers to be buyers.

Make good use of your driveway to display items.

Use your driveway. Put as much merchandise (stuff) as possible in the

---

Display Your Merchandise

driveway, especially large items, such as television sets, furniture, appliances, big toys, clothes racks, etc. Not only will this attract people driving or walking by, it will allow and encourage them to stop at the sale.

Hold your sale in the front of your house, if possible.

Your sale should be held in a garage in the front of your house, and on the driveway, if at all possible. Avoid having your sale in your backyard or inside the house. Why? It is hard to attract people to your sale if they cannot see the sale happening at all, let alone, see just how fabulous it is. Many safety-minded customers will not go into your house or your backyard, away from a more public eye. You should be similarly concerned with these kinds of safety or security issues also.

If you are having a garage sale, make it obvious to passersby.

Do not make people guess if you are having a sale or cleaning out your garage. Have accompanying signs or equipment to indicate that a sale, and a **great** one at that, is happening at your place.

Give customers room to shop.

Give people room to shop. In placing your clothes racks, tables, boxes and other stationary items, make sure that it is easy to get to an item. (Is it up too high or down too low?) Also, make sure that the shopper can maneuver around the merchandise without bumping into someone or something else.

Hang clothes if possible.

Hang as many of your clothes as possible on clothes racks. People seem to gravitate towards clothes racks (many shoppers go directly to the racks).

Display Your Merchandise

Clearly, it is easier for a shopper to look at your clothes on a rack, rather than from or on a table or box. Racks are more efficient for the seller as well; they maintain order and neatness (or the appearance of neatness). Given this preference, put your most expensive and best quality merchandise on the racks.

❖ Depending on your mechanical ability or the skills of your friends, you may want to consider making a clothes rack. Ask at the local hardware store for a simple plan, using pipe and standard fittings. Or you can use ladders, and suspend a rope or closet bars between them.

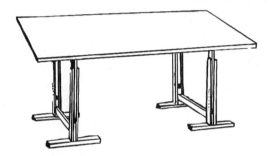

Use tables for breakable things.

Use tables for breakables, knickknacks, small appliances, toys, inexpensive clothes, and any other items that you want showcased with a minimum of touching.

Look at all of this GREAT stuff!

Display Your Merchandise

Use boxes for unbreakable things.	Use boxes for linens, inexpensive clothing, toy parts, stuffed animals, books, and any other items that invite touching. Box, as well, any merchandise that you will not mind being manhandled and ultimately destroyed.
Do not overload.	Do not overload or overstuff any clothes rack, box or table. If there is too much stuff on the rack, table or box, your shopper will likely be overwhelmed and will not look at all. Get another table, box or rack instead.
Consider grouping similar items together.	Consider the strategic location of your merchandise. Many retailers place their best bargains in the middle of the store. Others group items by type or kind.

For Your Notes...

Display Your Merchandise

OPTION 1   Garage Display (by type of container)

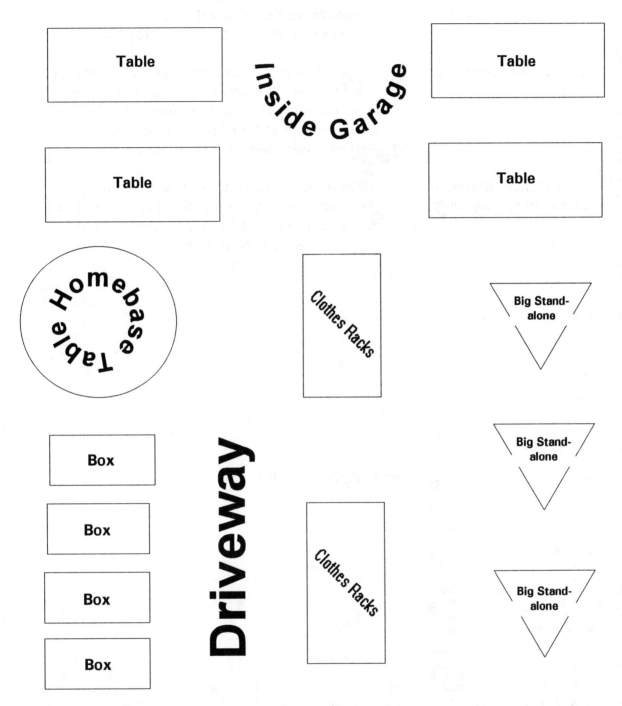

Big stand-alone items - large, bulky items that attract attention and you do not want to move again, such as televisions, furniture, appliances, big toys.

Tables - use for breakables, knickknacks, small appliances, toys, inexpensive clothes, any items you want highlighted without a lot of touching.

Boxes - use for linens, inexpensive clothes, toys, stuffed animals, books,

Display Your Merchandise

OPTION 2   Garage Display (by type of item for sale)

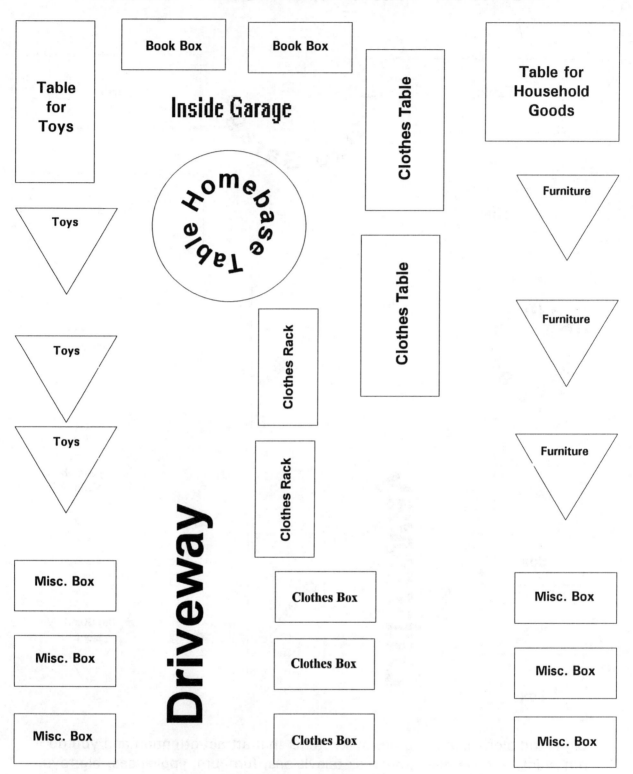

Big stand-alone items - large, bulky items that attract attention and you do not want to move again, such as televisions, furniture, appliances, big toys.

Tables - use for breakables, knickknacks, small appliances, toys, inexpensive clothes, any items you want highlighted without a lot of touching.

Boxes - use for linens, inexpensive clothes, toys, stuffed animals, books, and any other items that you want to be touched or don't care if they're touched or dropped.

Display Your Merchandise

For Your Notes...

Display Your Merchandise

E is for...

Educate your customer. Educate yourself.

There are definite benefits to shopping at a garage sale; educate your shopper about them.

Savvy, sophisticated garage sale shoppers clearly know and appreciate the benefits of garage sale shopping. More often than not, seasoned garage sale "professionals" do not need to be schooled on the values they are receiving from purchasing your stuff. It is this value that prompts their shopping (probably their obsession!) in the first place. The typical garage sale shopper, however, is not so skilled. You, the seller, have a unique opportunity to influence the outcome, and make a sale; you have the chance to point out just how great a deal the buyer could get.

Educate yourself first.

Before you can educate would-be buyers, you need to be educated yourself. You need to know how much an item costs retail, and you need to know how much an item will bring in at a garage sale.

There are several options to find out the

Educate Your Customer. Educate Yourself.

Learn retail costs.

cost of an item and to determine its retail worth. Try one or all of the following:

Price the item at a retail store.

1. Call a discount store (such as Walmart, Kmart, Target, etc.) and ask what the retail price is of the item you have to sell. Then call a moderately priced department store (such as Montgomery Wards, Sears, J.C. Penney, etc.) for the same information. Continue comparison shopping with a call to a more upscale department or specialty store (such as Saks, Bloomingdales, Macys, Dillards, Toys R Us, etc.). This should present you with a range of prices for the particular item.

Depend on your own judgement.

2. Rely on your own shopping experience and background. If you shop often, especially for a kind or category of goods (such as housewares), do not overlook the information you have already learned by your own shopping.

Check newspaper ads and catalogues for prices.

3. Look up prices in current newspaper ads or sales brochures and current and old catalogues (pack rats now have a legitimate reason to save this stuff). The J.C. Penney, Spiegel and Service Merchandise catalogues are invaluable resources.

Educate Your Customer. Educate Yourself.

The garage sale price is a percentage of retail price.

All things being equal (and often they are not...see the variables below), your merchandise should be priced as a percentage of the original cost. (Typical prices are set out within the letter, "P," "Pricing.")

If it is in good condition, charge more.

1. Condition affects price. The better the condition of your merchandise, the more likely you will get top dollar for it. Similarly, the worse the item looks, the less money you will sell it for at the sale. (See, for example, how cars are valued in the NADA Used Car Guide.)

2. The cleaner and neater an item is, the higher you can price it.

I won't forget ... I can charge more if my merchandise is in good shape!

If it is rare, charge more.

3. Availability will impact the price. The rarer an item is, the greater its worth should be. Example: antiques.

If it is popular, you can charge more.

4. Popularity will impact price. The more popular an item is, the more likely a buyer will pay for it. Example: expensive baby equipment.

If it is new, you can charge more.

5. If the item is unopened or you have a box for it, you can charge more for it.

Educate Your Customer. Educate Yourself.

It may be helpful to note the original cost.

There is often an advantage in putting a note on the item to indicate its retail cost. An advertisement (especially a recent one) showing the item and its sale price is usually very effective in alerting a buyer about the value of the potential purchase.

Warning: You probably should not put the retail price on everything in your sale. Reserve it for the more expensive items or the goods less known. You can presume that your shoppers know the general value of most everyday items.

For Your Notes...

Educate Your Customer. Educate Yourself.

F is for...

Flaunt fashion and flair.

Put your fashion sense to use at your sale.

Any fashion sense which a seller has may be put to good use at a garage sale, especially with respect to clothes.

Take time to match items.

Consider taking the time to pair items together which match, even if they are not sets. For example, put a shirt with a blazer, or place a turtleneck underneath a child's jumper. Add matching socks to an infant's one-piece outfit. Put a barrette or bow along a frilly dress.

Use your imagination.

By ready-making an outfit or ensemble for a buyer, you have increased the probability of sale. You may have stirred the buyer's own imagination or made the buyer realize what they already own to go with your sale item.

Be flexible.

Do not force, however, the buyer to buy the items as a set. Put a note on the goods, reading, "Buy separately or as a set." Set a better price if the buyer purchases both items. ($1.50 each piece or $2.50 for the set.)

Increase sales potential by pairing items together.

Often in putting separates together, you are able to sell your less expensive (and less desirable) items. If you put a pair of socks, valued at a quarter (of limited interest), with a pair of kid's overalls, you generally increase the appeal and attractiveness of the trousers (the more expensive item), and you have sold the less costly one.

To exaggerate this recommendation, consider even pairing an item which is unsellable (or marginally sellable) with another, minimizing the flaw of the unsellable item. For example, let's say a shirt has a spot or hole in the stomach area.   It is really not wearable as is. It is perfectly workable and functional, however, underneath a matching sweater. (Be careful here, though. You do not want to be deceptive or fraudulent in any way. You want your buyers to get a great deal and to come back to your sales, year after year.)

Many marketing gimmicks flaunt fashion and flair.

There are many marketing gimmicks which can help you sell your garage sale stuff. These are listed under chapter "P," for "Pricing."

For Your Notes...

Flaunt Fashion and Flair

G is for...

Get going!

*Start somewhere.
Get GOING!*

In order to make your sale a reality, you need to start somewhere. You cannot, will not, make a dime as a garage sale seller, if you do not have a sale. "But," you say, (especially after reading this entire book), "there is a lot to remember, and there is a lot of work to do." True enough, but it is all very workable, very do-able, particularly if you get going!

Don't put it off.

Most simply stated, avoid procrastination. Try not to wait until the last minute to begin preparing for your sale. Leave yourself a leisurely two or three weeks to get it all together.

*Start by doing
something you like.*

Start somewhere, anywhere, as long as what you do is calculated to lead to having a garage sale. It is easier to start with something that you like. (Examples: if you like to clean, start with your closet or basement. If you like fashion, pair outfits. Etc.)

Start small.

Start small. Do the most simple or menial of chores first until the momentum or swing of it motivates you further. (Examples: gather bags and hangers, pick out a corner to stockpile your stuff, etc.)

Practice your bargaining skills.

Practice garage sale skills in a non-garage sale setting. (Examples: Try to bargain for goods and services. Try with an airline. "Is that your best price? Is there any way to lower that price?" Go to a retail store with a marketing eye. Make change with your kids, etc.)

Become a buyer.

Get a first hand taste and experience of garage sales by becoming a buyer yourself. (That means you have to buy at these sales!) Practice your selling skills, in reverse as a buyer, including negotiating. See what you liked as a buyer and what you did not. Try to figure out why you had these likes and dislikes. Get a true sampling by attending at least 10 different sales. If time is at a premium, go to one large subdivision or neighborhood sale.

Refer to the timeline.

A timeline is often helpful to streamline your garage sale. One is set out on the following page.

Get Going!

58

3 or more weeks before the sale:
- Begin investigation and research.
- Buy supplies.
- Gather bags, boxes and hangers.
- Review ads. Learn lingo.
- Figure out when to have your sale.
- Figure out where to have the sale (if your place is less than ideal.)
- Clear space in your garage, basement or otherwise to gather your garage sale merchandise.
- Decide what things or kinds of things you will sell.
- Decide if you have enough stuff to sell or if you need co-sellers.
- Begin stockpiling your goods.
- Familiarize yourself with garage sale rules.
- Zero in on your goals.
- Read (or finish reading) this entire handbook.
- Check out the "legalities." Call local governments about any ordinances and laws. Plan to make any necessary arrangements. Verify you have insurance coverage with your agent.   Get any needed permits.

2 or more weeks before the sale:
- Call about rentals, tables, racks, etc.
- Call newspapers for their ad requirements (rates and deadlines).
- Continue and refine your investigation and research.
- Practice negotiation.
- Go to other garage sales.
- Continue to gather your goods.
- Clean your house in the preparation process (if you have the energy or stamina!).
- Begin to clean and dust your garage sale stuff.
- Get your staff lined up.
- Hire a baby-sitter for your kids.
- Familiarize yourself with pricing issues.
- Begin pricing anything that you have set aside for the sale.
- Write your ad, or at least get started with it.
- Follow through on anything from last week, especially any "legalities."

One or more weeks before the sale:
- Work on pricing. Label and price everything.
- Organize as you price. Put like items together.
- Hang and fold your merchandise as you price it.
- Review the copy for your ad. Edit it and plan to go forward with it.
- Continue to clean and dust your stuff.
- Place you ad (if you have to place it this early to make deadlines.)
- Follow through on anything remaining from the past weeks.

Get Going!

3 days before the sale:
- Plan your display and layout for the sale.
- Place your ads (only if it was okay to wait this long).
- Get your tables, racks, boxes, etc. to your garage.
- Make signs.
- Make sure all your goods are ready and available for sale.
- Clean garage.
- Finish pricing.
- Follow through on anything remaining from past weeks.

2 days before the sale:
- Begin to set up the sale. Make any tables, racks, etc.
- Continue to price, clean, etc, if necessary.
- Follow through on anything remaining from the past weeks or days.

1 day before
the sale:
- Complete any set up, including organizing and placing those items which will be placed outside of the garage once the sale starts
- Arrange your supplies for the day of the sale, including record keeping and money related supplies.
- Have friends over for preview (if you want to and can handle it.)
- Have plan for bad weather in place.
- Get cash.
- Put up your signs and banners (at night.)
- Confirm with your baby-sitter and helpers.
- Make sure ad appeared correctly.
- Try to get a good night's sleep.
- Review rules and expectations.
- Make breakfast and lunch or breakfast and lunch arrangements for tomorrow.
- Follow through on anything remaining from past weeks and days.

Day of sale:
- Put up signs if you did not do that last night.
- Move your car, down the street.
- Remember what you have learned. Use it.
- Get up early, at least an hour and a half before your sale is scheduled to begin.
- Bring all necessary supplies with you that are not already in place (ex: your cash).
- Have breakfast and lunch available for you and your helpers.
- Watch and learn. If something is not working, adjust.
- Straighten up as the day goes on.
- Have fun. Enjoy yourself and your customers.
- Clean up at the close of your sale, depending on your energy or inclination.
- Remove your signs.
- Tally your profits and rejoice!

Get Going!

Day after sale:

- Organize your leftovers.
- Return borrowed or rented goods.
- Clean up and put stuff away.
- Using your handbook, take a moment to write down your thoughts and observations. Record what you thought worked or did not.
- Take a deep breath and begin to plan for your next sale.
- Pay your co-sellers.

For Your Notes...

Get Going!

H is for...

Host your sale with hospitality.

Treat your customers with respect.

The enemy is not invading your camp. The people entering your property are patrons, shoppers, customers. They should be treated as your guests, with open-arms, dignity, respect and courtesy.

Pretend you are a party host.

Pretend that you are hosting a very informal cocktail party, a picnic, a newcomers' meeting, a club gathering or the like. Pretend further that you do not know any of the people who have been invited and who will attend.

Treat your customers like you would like to be treated.

How would you act? Would you post signs, telling people not to smoke? Would you put up a poster that said "Not responsible for accidents."? Would you let people know that if they break anything, they bought it? Of course not. You would expect your guests to follow a certain code of conduct or protocol, and, in **99.9%** of the cases, your expectations would be met.

The same expectations will probably be

Host with Hospitality

People generally follow the rules.

realized at your garage sale. People generally know the rules and follow them. People are not ordinarily rude or nasty either. There is no need to treat them that way.

Keep away from posting certain signs.

Do not greet your garage sale guests with any of the following signs (all of which we have personally seen, to our taste, insult and offense...talk about setting an unfriendly tone!):

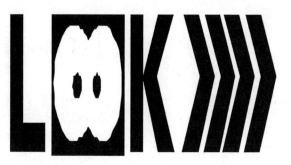

❖ Not responsible for accidents. (But see the warning at M, Miscellaneous.)

❖ Shop at your own risk. (But see the warning at M, Miscellaneous.)

❖ If you break it, you bought it.

❖ No smoking.

❖ No refunds or exchanges.

❖ No checks.

❖ All prices are firm.

❖ All sales are final.

❖ Sale opens at 8:00 a.m. prompt. Keep out until then.

❖ No exceptions!

Do not hover over the customer.

Leave your customer alone. Let the shopper browse and touch without any interference from you. (Remember how you feel when you walk into a store and a clerk rushes to "help you." Don't you ask for help if you need it? If your shopper is looking for something specific, he or she will probably ask.)

Be friendly.

Be Friendly. Make Conversation. Smile. Have fun. Enjoy yourself.

For Your Notes...

Host with Hospitality

I is for...

Investigate and research.

Knowledge and preparation will pay off.

As with every venture, especially a money-making one, being knowledgeable and prepared will pay off.

Reading from "A" to "Z" of this book is most of your research.

Each and every letter of the "garage sale alphabet" is, in effect, your general investigation and research. When you read and re-read this book you are conducting a majority of your investigation and research.

Personalize your research.

Try to personalize the general investigation and research within the pages of this book and gain your own framework and perspective.

Visit other garage sales.

One of the easiest way to personalize your investigation and research is to visit other garage sales and observe.

❖ See how the merchandise is priced.

❖ See how the goods are displayed and organized.

❖ See how the money is collected.

Pay attention to details.

❖ See whether the seller negotiates.

❖ Take it all-in...all the smells, sights and sounds.

❖ Judge what works for you as a shopper, a potential buyer, and why. What did you like? What did you not care for?

❖ What improvements could you make?

A subdivision or neighborhood sale is an especially good indicator. There will be seasoned sellers participating as well as "rookies" or one-timers. (One timers are those sellers who are offering their goods for sale because it is so easy to do when the whole neighborhood is participating; the seller just has to open up the garage without any advertising and the buyers will appear.)

The more you investigate and research, the more ideas will develop. Continue with your research.

Investigation and research is how hints, suggestions, and ideas (yours and those within this book) develop and continue to develop. Do not be afraid to continue with your research.

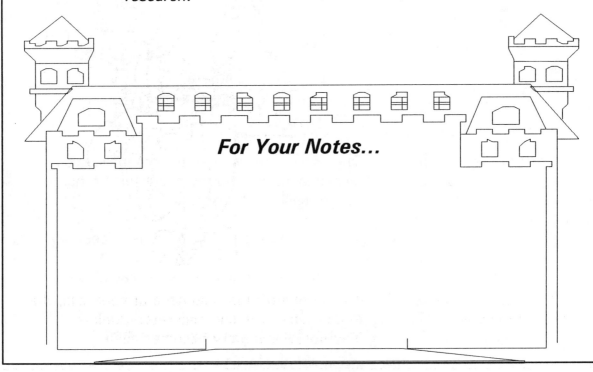

For Your Notes...

J is for...

Judge "junk" differently; redefine it.

There is no such thing as "junk."

There really is no such thing as junk. The cliché becomes especially true and real in the garage sale arena: one person's junk is another's treasure.

"Junk" is inventory. Include it in your sale.

You are encouraged to put each and every item of stuff in your sale, even things you would have called "junk" before you became a savvy garage sale seller. If you think an item is totally worthless, throw it in a nickel or quarter box, and laugh your way to the bank.

The more you have, the more you will sell.

The more stuff that you have at your sale, the more money you can generate. Junk is inventory. Inventory becomes cash.

Redefine "Junk"

If you have not used an item in one year or more, sell it. (This is especially true of clothes.) If no one has asked about an item that has been stored for more than one year, get it out of storage and sell it.

Let the buyers judge what is "worthless junk."

Try to remember just how creative people can and will be (explaining, beyond simple differences in taste, how and why something is junk to one person and not to another). For example, a buyer may happily purchase incomplete puzzles, because she will use them to decorate with (barrettes, pillows, picture frames, etc.); another buyer gets jeans and other clothes of unique fabric (regardless of condition) for making quilts; still another buyer finds items for theme parties (sixties, beach, etc.). Many people, professionals and amateurs, buy otherwise useless, "junk," items for parts, with endless possibilities (from bicycles to electronic equipment to toys).

There are no bounds to a shopper's creativity.

Your bits and pieces are my treasures...

What "junk" sells best?

Most sellers want to know what "junk" sells best. All "junk," as redefined, can be great sellers, depending on your advertising, marketing, display, pricing, etc.

Redefine "Junk"

If you must have a list of good sellers, use this one (but please use it with a "grain of salt."):

Antiques
Anything brand new
Baby equipment
Bicycles
Books
Clothing (designer or brand names)
Collectibles
Electronics
Furniture
Household items (including knickknacks)
Jewelry
Kids' stuff (clothes, toys, books)
Kitchen stuff (including dishes, glassware)
Maternity items
Sporting goods
Tools

Remember that you are organizing your life by selling your "junk."

Always remember that by selling your "junk," you are cleaning your own house and organizing your life.

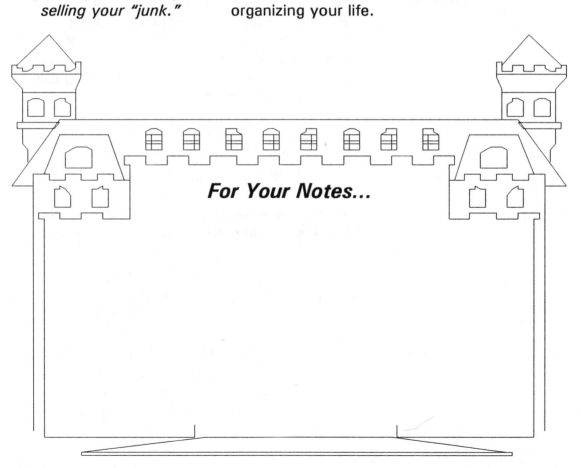

For Your Notes...

Redefine "Junk"

K is for...

Kid-proof and/or kid attract (Kid related suggestions)

Make the most of shoppers who have children.

A significant number of garage sale shoppers come with children. You can and should capitalize on this fact and use it to your best advantage.

Display items to invite or discourage touching.

Keep items that are of interest to a child where the child can see and touch them. In this way, a child might bring the item to the attention of their parent-shopper. Keep breakable items above child-level (viewing and reach). On the other hand, consider placing items that a child cannot harm on the ground, within a child's reach.

Expect children to play with toys.

Expect children to play with all your toys, no matter where located. If that upsets you, try to overlook it, considering it rather as a marketing ploy. Remember, the parent probably is noticing just how interested the kids are in that game or toy.

Kid-Proof and/or Kid Attract

Children playing with toys are not distracting mom or dad from buying.

Recognize too that if the children are busy with a particular toy, they are not tugging at mom or dad's "apron strings," urging the parent-shopper to leave. That usually translates into more money spent at your sale (the more time a shopper stays at your sale, the greater the chance that the shopper will buy something, or, better yet, a lot of things.)

Safeguard small pieces.

Headache Alert: Since you can expect children to play with your toys, and since your toys will be worth less if they are missing pieces, consider methods to safeguard small pieces. For example, tape key pieces of a toy directly on the box; put balls in a separate box, etc.

Consider having an area where children can play.

Take a lesson from giant, sophisticated marketers, which have areas for kids to play while their parents are shopping. Arrange for an area where the kids can play safely, without bothering their parents. If you are selling large toys, placing such goodies on the driveway is an ideal arrangement. If not, consider using your children's own, not-for-sale toys or borrowing a neighbor's kid's toys as an attraction. Just be sure to mark clearly that the items are not for sale.

Encourage your children to become involved.

Allow and encourage your own children to be involved with your sale. Indirect involvement is the key. Suggest that the children sell drinks (lemonade, soda/pop, etc.) and/or a snack (homemade cookies, brownies, etc.)

Hire a baby sitter if needed.

If your children are too young or too rambunctious to be involved with your sale, hire a baby-sitter.

Kid-Proof and/or Kid Attract

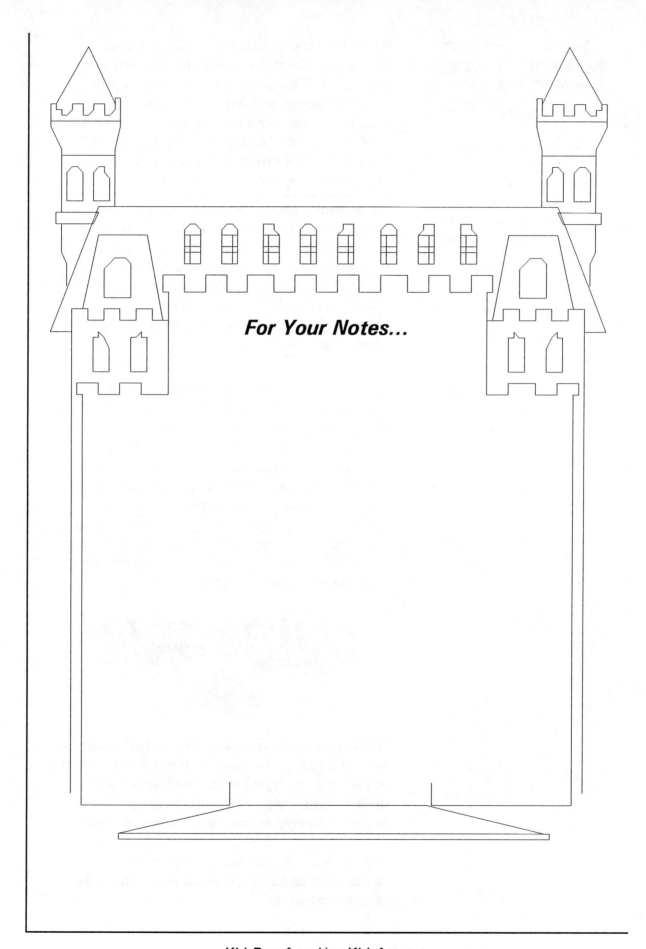

For Your Notes...

Kid-Proof and/or Kid Attract

L is for...

Live with the "Leftovers."

It is easy to handle "leftovers."

"Leftovers" are a necessary evil of a garage sale. All good garage sales will have leftovers, merchandise which simply did not sell. This is often frustrating for sellers. Having worked so hard at the sale, the idea of putting your stuff away is more than many can handle. But, do not despair. There are many, sensible, easy ways to handle leftovers.

You can minimize what is left.

Remember that, at least to some extent, you may be able to minimize leftovers with your own bargaining and negotiation during the sale.

Sell at any price!

If you want to get rid of all items, this philosophy should underline your bargaining tactics. ***Sell the item at any price.***

Be comfortable with decisions you make.

On the other hand, if an item (which was the subject of price haggling during the sale) remains at the end of the sale, you can remain comfortable that you chose this result. In other words, when you negotiated and bargained without making a sale, you decided, in effect, that it would be better not to sell the item at the bidder's price. You decided, in effect, that you would rather keep it or give it away. Try to remember this when dealing with the item as a leftover. (See also the letters, "Z" - Zero in on your goal and "B" - Bargain and Negotiate, for a more thorough discussion of these issues.)

Call back dealers who came to your sale.

It is not uncommon for "professionals," such as antique dealers, second-hand furniture retailers and other re-sellers, to offer to return at the end of your sale and buy a certain good or kind of goods. They will give you a fraction on the dollar of the merchandise's retail worth, offering you as little as ten percent of what you asked for the item at your sale. In turn, they will re-sell the item. It is a good idea for you to take the dealer's business card and call after the sale. Invite the dealer to bid on the item and consider, once again, whether to sell it to this re-seller. Recognize that your negotiating power at this point is somewhat shakier. If you make a deal, confirm that the dealer will arrange for pick-up.

Sometimes other shoppers will place bids on things. Call them back..

Other shoppers may offer a bid on an item as well. If you were organized enough to have kept that person's name and telephone number, it is worth it to call and find out if they are still interested in the item and on what terms. This method is only slightly effective; chances are limited that both parties will still be interested in making the deal without considerable negotiating on your part.

For most leftovers, decide and evaluate what is left and why. Then you can dispose of the leftovers properly.

For most leftovers, you need to evaluate what is left and why. This will allow you to decide what to do with each particular leftover.

Live with "Leftovers"

There are essentially, then, four remaining options for leftovers:

❖ Throw it away,

❖ Give it to Charity,

❖ Keep it (for yourself or for another garage sale)

❖ Consign it.

Recycle Unsold Items...

Throw it away if...

Throw it away if :

1. You were inclined to throw out the item before the sale, but took a chance;

2. No one ever looked at the item during the sale; the item is damaged, broken, irreparable, etc.;

3. You cannot bear the thought of ever seeing the item again and you would be embarrassed to give it to charity.

Consign it if...

Consign it if:

1. The item is the kind and type that a consignment store carries (for example, clothes fit this category, but artwork may not);

Live with "Leftovers"

2. If the item is in excellent or perfect condition, depending on the standards of the local consignment store owners;

3. The item is clean, neat, pressed, etc., again, depending on the standards of the local consignment store owners;

4. You have the time and energy to bring the merchandise to the consignment store, and can live with their prices;

5. You thought the item should have sold; you reasonably believe that the item did not sell because its price was "too high" for most garage sale shoppers, yet its price would be "right" for consignment shoppers;

6. You are inclined to try to sell it yourself at the next sale, but do not want to store it; the item is season-sensitive, with less chance of sale at your garage sale (for example, it is hard to sell winter coats in July);

Consign it if you really need the money.

7. If you really want or need to maximize your money.

Additional hints if you choose to consign: Call several consignment stores to see how each operates. Percentages between the owner of the store and consignor may differ from store to store, as will the term or the length of the consignment. As well, it is important to know the store's policy if the consigned merchandise does not sell by a certain date. Some stores ask you to pick up the merchandise, enabling you to then give it to your favorite charity, throw it away, or try to sell it again at a greatly reduced price.

Live with "Leftovers"

Keep it if...

Keep it if:

1. The item does not fall within the throw-away or consignment category.

2. You do not object to the storing of the item.

3. You plan on having another garage sale within a year.

4. Your beliefs and experience indicate that this item will sell and does sell usually.

Give it to charity if...

Give it to charity if:

1. The item does not fall within the throw-away, consignment, or keeper categories.

2. You do not want to pack, box or store the item.

3. You feel strongly about the purpose and goal of an organization in need of donations.

4. It would be to your financial and/or

spiritual benefit to donate to charity rather than receive cash for the items at a later date (at another sale or from the consignment store). Note, remember to ask for and keep your receipts for tax purposes.

Special consideration: Tax advantages may prompt your choice for leftovers - the charitable donation.

There may be a distinct tax advantage to you to donate your leftovers to charity. If, after you consult with a tax professional, you determine that it is to your benefit to donate items to charity, be sure that you make and keep the necessary records to support any deduction you might claim on your tax return. (Your tax professional can and should tell you what records to make and keep.) Work with your tax professional now.

Itemize and record.

Often, it is very difficult to figure out the value of your charitable donation on April 14, at tax time, especially when you held your sale the May before, some 11 months previous. As directed by your tax professional, you will probably need to take the time to write down and itemize each and every article you gave to charity after the sale and specify a value for each thing donated. We understand that valuation is or can be tricky, according to IRS standards.

You may need to determine value.

The IRS generally provides for deduction of the "fair market value" of an item, that is, what it would sell for in a thrift shop, its "thrift sale value." The IRS does not list specific values for items donated to charity in its publications or audit manual. You may need to determine yourself, with your tax professional, of course, what thrift shop value is on your particular item(s). Tax professionals are keenly aware of thrift shop value and probably have on hand a list of values from some local thrift stores for your use.

❖ If you donate $250.00 or more to a charity, you need to get a "written acknowledgment" from the charity, describing what was given. (Discuss with your tax professional what has to be stated on the "written acknowledgment.")

❖ If you donate more than $500.00, you need to file a specific form for "Non cash Charitable Contributions," form 8923. (See your tax professional for details, once again.)

Think of your sale as recycling.

Think of your sale as a form of recycling. Try to keep that in mind when distributing leftovers (and when making sales.)

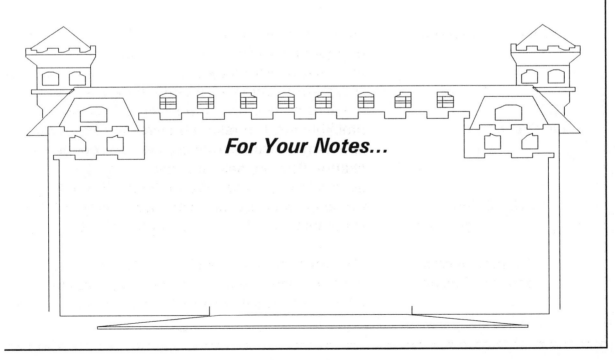

For Your Notes...

Live with "Leftovers"

M is for...

Master the Miscellaneous

There are more miscellaneous hints and suggestions.

As comprehensive and broad as the "garage sale alphabet" appears, a miscellaneous, catch-all category of information is needed. Here are some additional, otherwise not mentioned, thoughts:

There are many names for garage sales. These vary by region.

It is said that a rose by any other name would smell as sweet. Translation: there are many names for garage sales. These include garage sales, yard sales, rummage sales, and tag sales. The difference appears to be regional and no more; it is similar to calling "Coca-Cola$_{TM}$" soda, pop, tonic or soda pop.

Don't block the view...

Block your driveway.

Block your driveway with merchandise, boxes or otherwise to disable or stop any shoppers from parking in your driveway.

Be kind to your neighbors.

Be courteous to your neighbors. Do not traipse on their lawns; do not block their driveways; do not disturb them.

Identify yourself as the person in charge.

It is frustrating and confusing for a shopper to not know who to pay or who to ask for information. Eliminate this problem. Identify yourself as the seller. Wear a badge or name tag that says "THIS IS MY SALE." You can identify yourself by name, if you choose. Example: "I'm Sue. This is my sale." or "Sue-seller." If you don't like badges, you can identify yourself as a seller by what you wear. Putting on an apron, with pockets for your garage sale tools, is an easy way to show you are the seller.

You can also identify yourself with matching baseball-type hats or identical badges or name tags.

> **It is easier for the customers if they can quickly identify you as the seller...**

The IRS does not require you to pay taxes on the dollars you make at your sale.

IRS rules do not require you to pay income tax on the money you make at your sale, in the majority of cases. Your profits aren't treated as income (upon which you would have to pay taxes), as long as the amount you sell an item for is less than what you paid for the item. In other words, you are selling at a loss, as far as the IRS is concerned. Similarly, It is not necessary to collect sales tax. (You are cautioned to contact the IRS or a tax advisor or professional to verify this information and its applicability to you.)

TAKE A PEEK AT THIS...

Consider adding more merchandise as the sale continues.

Some people fill in (add, as needed) more merchandise as their sale continues. If you are going to do this, make mention of it in your ad, stating "new items each day." Also, put up signs in your garage saying this. Otherwise, shoppers may think that what you have to sell on the second day is less desireable, and more picked-over. It is a presumption which discourages shoppers from coming to your sale on the second or third day, or from buying on those days.

Let there be music...

Play music.

Some sellers believe there to be an advantage to having music on during the sale. This is especially true if you are trying to sell a radio or stereo. It applies to appliances for sale as well. There is an advantage to having a TV or computer running.

Keep an eye on your pets.

Do not let your pets get under foot where they can hurt shoppers or frighten them. (Do you know how many people are afraid of dogs and cats?) Do not allow your pets to get loose and distract you from the sale. (How can you handle the sale if you are running around the neighborhood calling Rover? What if a shopper hits frolicking Rover in the street?) The safest course...ask someone else to watch your animals for the day or board them if necessary.

Master the Miscellaneous

Check with your insurance agent about liability issues.

Check with your insurance agent if there is any question of whether you are or would be responsible for accidents. Generally, for an occasional garage sale, homeowners' insurance should cover an accident, but you should find out for yourself from your own agent about your own circumstances and your own policy coverage.

Follow the rules...
Check to be sure no ordinances ban garage sales...

Check with your local governments about garage sale laws or ordinances.

Make sure that there are not any laws or ordinances (including fees) which govern how and when you may hold a garage sale. Call the city or town government in which you live and ask them.

Check with local homeowner's or condo or apartment associations about their rules also.

Make sure that there are not any rules in your homeowners associations, condominium or apartment organizations, which affect when and how you can hold a garage sale. Some very affluent subdivisions, for example, have neighborhood rules and conditions which forbid signs or garage sales altogether.

Master the Miscellaneous

*Pay attention to
security issues.*

Unfortunately, there are, or can be, security issues to deal with at your garage sale. Many of these have been discussed already. (See, for example, scam alerts relating to money under letter, "C;" recommendations regarding not allowing people in your house under letters, "D" and "T.")

No deception, fraud or trickery...

*Take simple
precautions.*

Use good, sound judgment in dealing with people, and, definitely take simple precautions.

Lock all the doors to your house, not just the doors leading to the garage.

Do not flash your money around at the sale.

Do not count your money in front of people at the sale.

Do not brag about how much money you have made, or are making, even if someone asks you how it is going. (If someone asks how it is going, say, "just fine," or "as expected.")

*Keep an eye on your
sale.*

On the theory that there is safety in numbers, have a helper with you at all times, to minimize the possibility of foul play.

*Have helpers and a
phone around to
minimize foul play.*

Keep a cordless telephone in the garage for security and as a customer convenience. Do not announce personal information about yourself at your sale. (We have actually heard sellers announce that they live alone, or that they were going on vacation next week.)

Walk around and watch your shoppers. Stay alert and be visible; a person is less likely to take something from your sale if he or she can be seen.

Is there shoplifting at a sale? Probably yes.

Our philosophy about shoplifting is this. If someone needs something that you have at your garage sale badly enough to steal it, they can have it. While shoplifting is horrible, and not condoned at all, you have to remember where you are (a garage sale) and what you are trying to accomplish (get rid of your stuff, making the most money you can.) Again, you can lessen the chances of stealing if you are around, if you are watching your stuff and keeping alert.

Dress for success.

Wear comfortable clothes and shoes/sneakers at your sale. You will have to be able to move, bend and stretch; sit and stand for long periods of time and you do not want to have to worry about whether your clothes got dirty during the sale (they will!). Do not forget that sunscreen either!

Use your handbook.

During and after your sale, using this book, take a moment to write down your thoughts and observations. Record what you thought worked or did not. It will be helpful for your next sale.

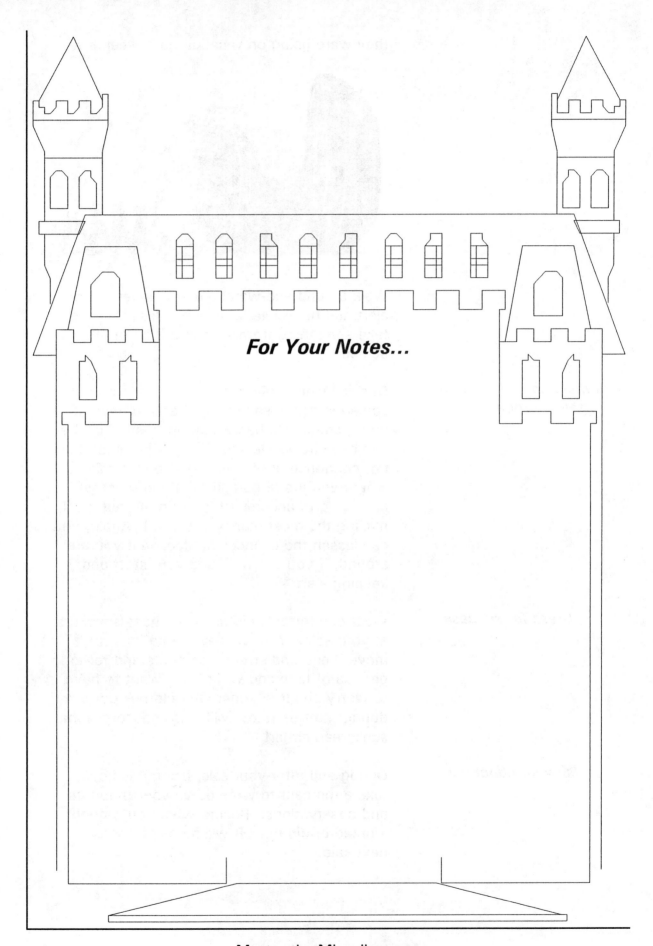

For Your Notes...

Master the Miscellaseous

N is for...

Notice Neatness; it counts.

Don't ignore neatness. It is important.

You should not ignore neatness and cleanliness just because your sale is being held in a garage. The old saying that neatness counts is especially true when having a garage sale. It is well worth your time to tidy up a bit. It is not necessary to be able to eat off the floor of the garage. However, you should do a quick sweeping of the floor, removing especially any chemicals or potentially unsafe conditions (such as an oil spill or glass breakage).

Make sure displays are neat and free from dirt.

Make sure that your display tables (actual or home-made substitute) are clear of dust, dirt and stains. If these cannot be eliminated (because of your time constraints or because the stains simply cannot be removed), drape a clean sheet or tablecloth over the display table before setting your merchandise down on the table.

You'll earn more with a neat sales area and clean merchandise... straight from the horse's mouth!

Dirty merchandise will not bring as much money.

Many shoppers, especially novice ones,

Notice Neatness

presume that if your merchandise is dirty, it is not worth looking at, or that it is not worth buying. Sometimes an item is so dirty that the buyer cannot figure out what it is. Other times, a shopper figures it is not worth the effort to clean the item, for you or for him/her, so the shopper walks away. In either event, you have lost a sale.

If an item is stained, it's damaged.

If you cannot remove a stain, from clothing or other goods, price the item as damaged. The value of an item is generally considered compromised by the damage.

Make different use of a stained item.

You may however be able to make a different use of the item or minimize its damage. For example, if you have a stain on a shirt, you can place it under a sweater, with little loss in value. (Be careful here. Don't be deceitful or misleading.)

Wash and iron clothes to earn more.

Consider washing and/or ironing any clothes before offering them for sale. As a shortcut, you can attain the smell of "clean" and a "pressed look" by putting your clothes in the dryer with a fresh dryer sheet.

Use cleaners to spruce up items.

The smart seller should note these common and very effective stain removers, for use on clothing and household items, including toys:

❖ Paste mixture of powder/crystal dishwashing detergent and vinegar, with or without bleach

---

Notice Neatness

* Vinegar

* Liquid bleach (apply with Q-Tip™ first to test colorfastness)

* Nail polish remover

* "Gum Out™"

* Ammonia

* Soft Scrub™ (for crayon)

* Dawn™ detergent (for removal of grease stains)

Be sure to straighten regularly.

You will probably need to straighten out your merchandise (especially those on tables) several times during each day of your sale.

For Your Notes...

Notice Neatness

O is for...

Organize your stuff.

Be organized.
You cannot go wrong being organized. If you have an orderly, functional, structured method of arranging and sorting your merchandise, it will be easier for you to make a sale.

Make things easy to find.
If your shoppers can see it, can find it without asking for your help, they are more likely to buy it.

A messy sale is stressful.
Mess creates stress, plain and simple. If you or your shoppers have to search and search for items, time and energy is wasted unnecessarily.

Make your sale user-friendly.
Do whatever is necessary (considering what you have to sell) to create an organized, user friendly, buying environment.

Get up early.
Get up early, at least an hour and a half before your sale is scheduled to begin.

Plan ahead.
Plan ahead in organizing your merchandise. Keep in mind that you need to fit everything in

Organize Your Stuff

the garage only if the weather is bad, or as an overnight storage place until your sale is held.

Store your stuff under tables to get ready to move outside.

Put all the merchandise which you intend to put outside (in the driveway or in the front yard) underneath the folding tables and/or in one section of the garage (such as the left corner). This way you can direct others to help you move the stuff, with little involvement on your part.

Make sure there is plenty of space for shoppers to shop.

Give people room to shop. In placing your clothes racks, tables, boxes and other stationary items, make sure that it is easy to get to an item. Is it up too high or down too low? If so, adjust.

Make sure that the shopper can maneuver around the merchandise without bumping into someone or something else. The space between racks, tables, etc. should be at least the width of two average people.

If you have a lot of a certain kind of merchandise, further organize and separate to make it more organized. Examples: If you have a lot of books, group by kind of book, such as romance, mystery, popular, children, etc.

Group similar items together.

Group items by type or kind. Example: put all housewares together in one area; put all clothes together in one area, and so on, for

Organize Your Stuff

toys, linens, books, etc.

Sort clothes by size.

For clothes, group by gender (boy/girl, men/women) and then by size.

You can also group by price. Example: everything in this box is 25 cents.

Hang as many clothes as you can.

Hang as many of your clothes as possible on clothes racks. People tend to gravitate towards clothes racks (many shoppers go directly to the racks). Clearly, it is easier for a shopper to look at your clothes on a rack, rather than from, or on, a table or box. Racks are more efficient for the seller as well; they maintain order and neatness (or the appearance of neatness). Given this preference, put your most expensive and best quality merchandise on the racks.

Use tables for breakables.

Use tables for breakables, knickknacks, small appliances, toys, inexpensive clothes, and any other items that you want showcased with a minimum of touching.

Use boxes for items which will be touched alot and may be destroyed.

Use boxes for linens, inexpensive clothing, toy parts, stuffed animals, books, and any other items which invite touching. Box as well any merchandise that you will not mind being manhandled and possibly destroyed.

Do not overload.

Do not overload or overstuff any clothes rack, box or table. If there is too much stuff on the rack, table or box, your shopper will likely be overwhelmed and will not look at all. Get another table, box or rack instead.

Organize Your Stuff

Keep children's things where children can see them.

Keep items that are of interest to a child where the child can see and touch them, so that they might bring the item to the attention of their parent-shopper.

Keep breakable things out of childrens' reach.

Keep breakable items above child-level (viewing and reach). On the other hand, consider placing items that a child cannot harm on the ground, within a child's reach.

Consider where you put your merchandise (its strategic location). Layout can be helpful in selling your merchandise. It helps set the tone of your sale and should attract passerbys, drivers or walkers, to stop, browse and buy.

> NOTE: Take a lesson from giant, sophisticated marketers, which have areas for kids to play while their parents are shopping. Arrange for an area where the kids can play safely, without bothering their parents. If you are selling large toys, placing such goodies on the driveway is an ideal arrangement. If not, consider using your children's own not-for-sale toys, or borrowing a neighbor kids' toys as an attraction.
> Just be sure to mark clearly that the items are not for sale.

Use your merchandise to attract customers.

The middle of your area is the most sellable.

Many retailers place their best bargains in the middle of the store. Put your best merchandise (most sellable) in the middle of the driveway.

Organize Your Stuff

Put as much as you can in your driveway.	Put as much merchandise as possible in the driveway, especially large stand-alone items, such as television sets, furniture, appliances, large toys, clothes racks, etc. Not only will this attract people driving or walking by, it will enable and encourage them to stop at the sale.

Empty the garage.	Leave as little as possible in the garage, unless the weather warrants it.
Keep breakables safe.	Keep breakables in the garage. You want the breakable items to be as safe as possible.
Line your driveway with boxes.	Line the sides and front of the driveway with boxes.
Label everything.	Label _everything_ with a price. This will aid in your organization tremendously. (See "P," "Pricing," for additional information and insight in this area.) Label everything in your garage sale which is not for sale also. Simply put masking tape on the item reading "Not for Sale." Alternatively, rope off and separate the stuff in your garage which you are not selling. Separate with rope, twine, string, sheets, or black plastic. Put up a sign stating that these goods are not for sale.
State if specific things are not for sale.	
Make a table your home base.	Consider having a table with your garage sale tools on it (see "T") as a "homebase" during the sale. You can make change here, check out the merchandise, keep all your needed supplies together in one spot and just rest, if needed. Place the table directly in front of the garage, between the goods within the garage and the merchandise on the driveway.

Organize Your Stuff

Organization makes dealing with leftovers easier.

There is a hidden benefit to all this organization as well. In the event that you have leftovers (see "L"), you have minimized the amount of time that you have to spend putting things away. You can just box all like items together for future handling. (Example: all household goods, all clothes size 10, etc.)

Organize the sale throughout the year.

Organize during the year as well, in anticipation of an upcoming, future sale. When you have decided to replace something or when you have determined that a clothing item no longer fits, mark it for sale at that time and put it in a storage area in your garage, basement, etc., for your annual garage sale.

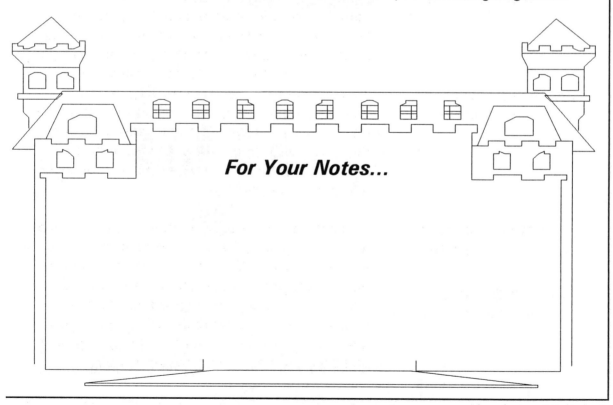

For Your Notes...

Organize Your Stuff

P is for...

Price everything and price it fairly.

Label everything clearly.

Every item at your sale should be clearly marked with a price tag or label. The tag or label should state the dollar amount of the item and any other necessary identifier, such as your initials, a description of the item or the like (Example: Book $1.00 JW; or $1.00; or $1.00 JW). The tag should be simple and not damage your item. Do not write in pen or in permanent marker on any item directly. (Example: don't write in ink on the front or spine of a book; don't write $1.00 in permanent marker on the clothes tag.)

Labeling discourages price switching.

If you identify your item when you price it, you will lessen the chance that an underhanded shopper will try to switch tags for a better price. (Ex: A tag reading "Picone dress $10.00, JB" cannot be switched with a

Price Everything

tag reading "Basic dress $3.00 Val.")

Pricing will save you time.

Pricing everything will save you tremendous time in the long run. ***How?***

There will be less questions and less memory recall.

1. You will not have to answer repeated questions about how much an item costs.

2. You will not have to rely on your memory about how much an item costs, especially when your sale is very busy.

Shoppers don't like to ask prices.

3. Shoppers are often reluctant or scared off when prices are not stated, costing you a sale.

4. People do not like to guess at a price, costing you a sale.

If all items are priced, a shopper will probably buy more.

5. If a shopper does not ask the price, he or she is likely to leave the sale without buying anything. If a shopper knows the price of everything, he or she is likely to buy more. A shopper may not be interested in a book at $2.00, but may buy it at 25¢.

> **Making prices easy to read helps both you and your buyer, which is very good for your sale...**

Pricing leads to more realistic negotiations.

Pricing everything leads to more reasonable negotiating and bargaining. Example: Let us say that you are trying to sell a desk. You have tagged it at $25.00. Chances are that you will receive an offer somewhere between $15.00 and $20.00. If you had not priced the item, you could (and probably would) get an offer for as little as $5.00. It is a lot harder to negotiate when you are this far apart.

Label the same way for each item.

It is helpful to put your pricing labels or tags on the item at the same place for every item.

Price Everything

Always put your price in the top left corner of the item, or the bottom right corner, or the upper middle, etc. This way you can locate easily the price for a buyer. You can find the price easily when you are separating and adding up the prices for different participating sellers also.

Take the time to label your stuff...

Note- scam alert...Sometimes an underhanded buyer will try to switch price tags or labels. If you put the tags on your stuff in the same place on every item, you will recognize the system and a misplacement of a label, but the shopper probably will not. You will outfox the shopper.

Don't use your own label codes.

Avoid using your own labeling code or system. (Example: all yellow dots mean $.25, orange dots are $.50, blue dots are $1.00 and green dots are $2.00). *Why?*

If you can take the time to put a dot on an item, you can take the time to mark each dot with the item's price. (If you have to, establish your code and then mark the dots with the dollar amount of the item while the dots are on a piece of paper or sticky sheet

Price Everything

they came on in the package.) In other words, a labeling system does not really save you time, especially when you consider its disadvantages.

A personal pricing code is not easily understood by buyers.

While the labeling system seems easy for you, it is very hard for the shoppers to figure out or decipher. The would-be buyer is continually looking around for your price list, each and every time she or he picks up an item of interest. It can become so distracting and needlessly time-consuming for the shopper that often the shopper will leave in disgust or frustration.

A labeling system is not shopper-friendly.

A labeling system is not user or shopper-friendly. It hampers a buyer from quickly viewing your merchandise and purchasing it.

A buyer doesn't have the time to learn a code.

Most garage sale shoppers will "hit" or attend many sales on a particular day. Busy shoppers are not inclined to learn a new pricing system every time they go to another sale. It is not even-handed for you to expect them to do this.

There are exceptions to the "pricing rule."

> **Are there any exceptions to the "price it all" rule?**
> **Yes, as with any rule, there are exceptions.**

If you have no time at all....

If everything in a category is the same price, you may choose not to label each item.

If time is at premium, that is, if you have no time at all (and be real honest with yourself here!), you can price by categories. Examples: all clothes are $1.00 unless otherwise marked (and price the ones which are worth more than $1.00); all pants are $1.00, all shirts are .50, etc. If you do price this way, make a ton of signs to show your prices. If you do price this way, recognize too that you are minimizing your potential profits. How? You probably could get more money on many of the items that you have lumped together for your own ease. Example: Aren't there any shirts worth more than 50¢?

Price Everything

*Inexpensive boxed
items can go unpriced.*

As has been mentioned elsewhere, including at letters, "D" and "O," there are good reasons to box certain items. You do not need to individually price these items (that is, where the items in this box are .25 each), as long as you know what is in the box (so that when your shoppers are ready to pay for it, you will not be fumbling or wondering about the price).

*Strategy:
Price as high as you
can while still selling
goods.*

Since you want to make the most money you can, and maximize your profits, you are walking a fine line: you need to price as high as you can and still quickly sell your merchandise.

Fair pricing is critical.

Fair and precise pricing is a critical part of the garage sale process. If you overprice one item, it is easy for a shopper to think that you overpriced everything.

*Pricing is a learned
skill.*

Pricing, however, does not need to be an art; it can be a learned skill. There are many different theories about pricing. It is possible for each expert to have a different set of rules and standards. There are just so many variables. The good news about that is simple: do not worry about making mistakes. Just do your best, given what you have to work with, remembering that you did not really want to keep that item in the first, second or third place.

Price Everything

If in doubt, price it higher.

If you are in doubt about a price, price it slightly higher than you might otherwise mark it. Why? The hard fact is this: You can always come down on a price, but you cannot go up.

When pricing, remember retail.

To properly price, you need to know how much an item costs retail, and you need to know how much an item will bring in at a garage sale.

There are several ways to determine worth.

There are several options to find out the cost of an item and to determine its retail worth.

Check with retail stores.

Call a discount store (such as Walmart, Kmart, Target, etc.) and ask what the retail price is of the item you have to sell. Then call a moderately priced department store (such as Montgomery Wards, Sears, J.C. Penney, etc.) for the same information. Complete the comparison shopping with a call to a more upscale department or specialty store (such as Saks, Bloomingdales, Macys, Dillards, Toys 'R Us, etc.). This should present you with a range of prices for the particular item.

Rely on your own shopping habits.

Rely on your own shopping experience and background. If you shop often, especially for a category of goods (such as housewares), do not overlook the information you have already learned by shopping.

Price Everything

Check prices in catalogues.

Look up prices in current and old catalogues (pack rats now have a legitimate reason to save this stuff), newspaper ads or sales brochures. The J.C. Penney, Spiegel and Service Merchandise catalogues are excellent resources.

Visit other garage sales.

Visit other garage sales and see how the merchandise is priced. A subdivision or neighborhood sale is a good indicator. There will be seasoned sellers participating as well as rookies or one-timers, those sellers who are offering their stuff for sale because it is so easy to do so when the whole neighborhood is participating.

Visit thrifts.

You may want to visit thrift stores also to see how their merchandise is priced.

Prices should equal a specific percentage of retail.

All things being equal (and often they are not...check the variables below), your merchandise should be priced as a percentage of the original cost. Typical prices follow:

Price Everything

ITEM	% OF RETAIL
Clothing-adult	5-25%
Clothing-kids	5-33%
Clothing-maternity	10-33%
Furniture	5-25%
Toys	5-50%
Bicycles	10-33%
Household	5-25%
Bedding	5-10%
Exercise equipment	5-50%
Books	5-10%
Artwork	5-10%
Antiques/Collectibles	Special Rules-below
Appliances	5-25%
Electronics	5-25%
Tools	5-25%
Jewelry	5-25%

It is very difficult to make broad, sweeping generalizations about how to price. This explains (and rationalizes) why a range of prices have been given with a list of factors impacting the range.

There are certain factors which affect price.

Condition, availability and popularity affect price.

Generally, you can set your price as a percentage of the retail price, with several important warnings and exceptions:

Condition affects price. The better the condition of your merchandise, the more likely you will get top dollar for it. Similarly, the worse an item looks, the less money you will sell it for at the sale. (See for example how cars are valued in the NADA Used Car Guide.)

Availability will impact the price. The rarer an item is, the greater its worth should be. Ex., antiques.

Seasonal items sell better during or before the season. For example, it is easier to sell shovels and coats in the fall, and lawn mowers and bikes in the spring.

Popularity will impact price. The more popular an item is, the more likely a buyer will pay for it. Ex., expensive toys, baby equipment.

The cleaner and newer it is, the more you can charge.

The cleaner and neater an item is, the higher you can price it.

If the item is unopened or you have a box for it, you can charge more for it.

Namebrands increase price.

A designer label or namebrand will increase the price.

If it's out of date, charge less.

Out-of-date, obsolete items (such as record

Price Everything

players, 8 track tapes, typewriters, etc.) will not command a high price, except as collector's items, as antiques, or for parts.

If it's broken, charge less.

If the item does not work, and it should, it will be worth less. (You should say whether the item does not work, if you know. If you are asked and you do not know, say, "I do not know" and tell the shopper to presume it does not work.)

Collectibles and antiques are different.

There are different, special rules for antiques and collectibles. If you have any suspicion or inkling that a particular item is an antique or collectible, check it out before selling it. Don't be sorry. Find out its worth. Go to the library or book store for one of many guides on antiques and collectibles and their value. You can also call a professional appraiser for an estimate of value. Start with the yellow pages or contact organizations or associations dedicated to this field.

P.S. Many miscellaneous factors also affect price. Consider reviewing the suggestions at the letters, "F/Fashion," "K/Kid related information," and "Z/Zero in on your goal."

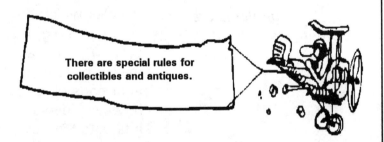

There are special rules for collectibles and antiques.

Price in greater increments..

Items should not be priced less than a nickel. No items should be priced for a penny. Most items are priced in quarter increments. This makes it much easier to add, without any sacrifice to the bottom line.

There are some things that are difficult, but not impossible, to sell.

There are certain items that are difficult (but not impossible) to sell, no matter how great a shape they are in:

Price Everything

Hygiene-related things are hard to sell.

Any items where people might question hygiene and doubt whether they should use the item second-hand. Examples: shoes, underwear, lingerie, bathing suits, sheets, towels, earrings.

Some baby clothes may be hard to sell.

Baby clothes from 0 to 6 months are sometimes hard to sell, even when they are in excellent condition. Most new parents have received a lot of this size from baby showers or, more likely, have realized that their infants are already too big for these sizes at birth!

Personal taste items are difficult to sell.

Articles which are very much a matter of personal taste are hard to sell. Example: artwork, unless you are pricing the frame itself.

Large items are sometimes difficult to sell.

Articles which are especially large and heavy (such as a big, brass bed) may be hard to sell). The average shopper does not have the means or tools (a delivery truck) to get the enormous piece to their home. (Note, however, dealers always appear to be interested in buying furniture.)

There are many marketing gimmicks.

There are many marketing gimmicks which you can and should use at your sale to sell more of your stuff. Consider, for example, these:

Have a box of free items.

Give your shoppers a paper bag or sack to fill with your garage sale merchandise. Tell your shoppers that each bag is $1.00 or $2.00, $5.00, or whatever, for the entire bag, no

Price Everything

matter what the shopper puts in the bag. You can expand or limit this... everything from this section or table can be put in a bag for a dollar, or, everything is included in the dollar bag deal except items marked, etc.

Reduce your prices every day of the sale.

Reduce your prices every day of your sale. Below is a suggested schedule:

Day one of the sale	Regular price
Day two of the sale	25% off
Day three of the sale	50% off
Day four of the sale	75% off

or

Day one of the sale	Regular price
Last day or	50% off
Day two of the sale	50% off

or

Day one	Regular price
Day two, last day	Everything $1.00 unless otherwise marked

The choices are unlimited. Make sure that you tell everyone what you are doing. Make

Price Everything

posters or signs and hand them out at your sale. Announce the mark downs every once in a while at the sale. State your markdowns in your ad.

> Note: you do not need to go around to each price and mark down the price itself. Take the markdown or reduction from the original price when they buy and pay. Your signs should say "Markdowns taken when you pay."

Practice pricing with the guide on the next page.

A shortcut practice guide (attached) should help you when pricing your stuff. It will help you price fairly, with a minimum of time on your part.

For Your Notes...

Price Everything

A Shortcut Pricing Practice Guide

1. Get a base, bottom line, price for each item of your merchandise. To do this, **take ten percent (10%)** of the **retail price** of the item:

   $_____$ (Retail price) x .10 = $_____$ (Base price)

   Example: A "Lenox" china vase costs $60.00 retail.
   Its base price is $6.00. ($60.00 x .10 = $6.00)

2. Adjust your price according to the specific value features of the item. To do this, **add five percent (5%)** of the **retail price** for added values:

   $_____$ (Retail price) x .05 = $_____$ (Value added price)

   Added values go beyond the basics, beyond the normal wear and tear. Below are some specific examples of added values.

   Add five percent (5%) if the item is in very good or excellent condition.
   Add five percent (5%) if the item is rare, but not an antique.
   Add five percent (5%) if the item is in high demand, or is popular.
   Add five percent (5%) if the item is especially clean and neat.
   Add five percent (5%) if the item is unopened, boxed, or brand new with tags.
   Add five percent (5%) if the item has a warranty or written instructions.
   Add five percent (5%) if the item has a designer label or name-brand manufacturer.
   Add five percent (5%) if the item has any other unique feature which increases its value.

   Example: If that "Lenox" china vase was a wedding present that you never
   opened, add 5% each for its excellent condition, its popularity, its newness
   with a box, and its brand name appeal, for a total of 20% additional.

3. Adjust the value given the faults of the item. To do this, **subtract/deduct five percent (5%)** of the **retail price** of the item.

   $_____$ (Retail price) x .05 = $_____$ (Reduced price)

   Reduced values go beyond the basics, beyond normal wear and tear. Below are some specific examples of reduced values.
   Subtract five percent (5%) if the item is in very bad or poor condition.
   Subtract five percent (5%) if the item is readily available, especially at garage sales.
   Subtract five percent (5%) if the item is rusty, very dirty, or has permanent stains.

Subtract five percent (5%) if the item does not work or is defective.
Subtract five percent (5%) if the item does not have a designer label or name-brand manufacturer.
Subtract five percent (5%) if the item is obsolete, outdated or old-fashioned.
Subtract five percent (5%) if the item has any other feature which decreases or lessens its value.

Example: If that "Lenox" china vase looks old-fashioned and holds only one flower, limiting its use, subtract 10%.

Subtract $6.00 ($3.00 from two categories) from the $18.00 above.
$18.00 - $6.00 = $12.00 asking price.

Important Footnote: Remember the ranges shown on Page 103. If the kind of item you are selling usually sells for more than 10% of retail, say 25% to 50% of its retail, you may want to reach a bottom line with 25% of the retail price, not 10%. The 10% standard used here is meant to be a general, safe, conservative, pricing approach, aimed at saving you time, but still allowing you to sell your stuff quickly and fairly, without giving it away.

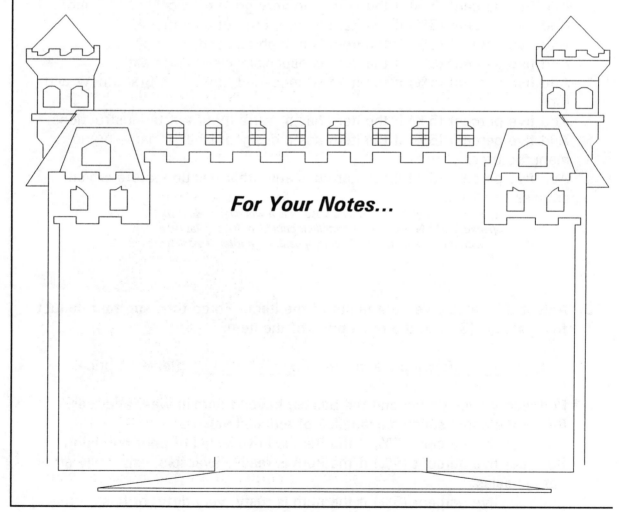

For Your Notes...

Price Everything

Q is for...

Quickly react

If you are not making sales, react and make changes.

Be careful not to use your research in a vacuum. In other words, you should not be a slave to what you have learned (in this handbook, from your own observations or otherwise), if what you have learned is not working at your sale.

You are probably puzzled at this point, wondering why the recommendations or guidelines you have gathered would not work. You must remember that it is not a perfect world. One idea may work better in a given market, or for a particular kind of item, or the like.

Some things are beyond your control.

Similarly, despite all your organized and methodical planning, some things are just beyond your control. For example, there could be a 30 degree, rainy/snowy day, at your September sale.

Pay attention to what is happening at your sale.

The key is recognizing what is working and what is not. To do this, you must pay attention to what is going on at your sale... what is selling and what is not; who is buying and who is not; what is being looked at and

Quickly React

111

what is not. Obviously, that means you will have to look and listen to your shoppers. When you see what your shoppers are doing, you will be able to react accordingly.

If adjustments are needed, make them.

If you need to make adjustments, make them. This may mean lowering your prices, pairing clothes to make outfits, moving your merchandise physically or the like.

Talk to your customers.

Do not hesitate to make conversation with your shoppers. Not only is it friendly and customer-oriented, it may give you valuable feedback about your sale.

For example, if someone picks up a vase and holds it in their hands while walking around your garage sale, you should expect that they will buy it. If you see them leaving the driveway without the vase, you should take the opportunity to say something. "Did you change your mind about the vase? If I lowered the price might you buy it?"

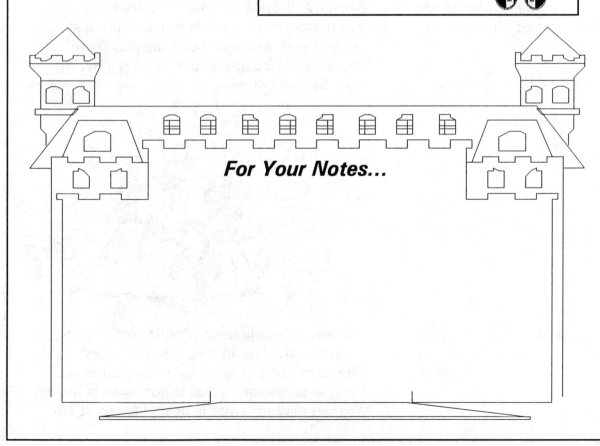

For Your Notes...

Quickly React

R is for...

Recognize the Rules and Rituals of Garage Sales.

There is an established code of conduct at garage sales.

There is definitely a code of conduct, an established standard, a habit of behavior, in sum, a set of rules under and by which most garage sale shoppers operate. It is often regarded as an insult or offense for a seller to ignore the rules. Most people, including garage sale shoppers, appreciate the fairness associated with rules and think it proper to follow them.

Shoppers generally know the rules.

Many of the people who attend garage sales are regulars. They have learned from their own, practical experience what to expect at a garage sale. They know what is standard operating procedure ("SOP").

Garage Sale "Regulars" have learned from experience...

The seller should recognize garage sale rules and play by them.

It is important for the seller to recognize garage sale rules and "SOP" for several practical, monetary reasons:

If you don't follow the rules, you look foolish and you will sell less.

A failure to pay attention to "SOP" makes you appear a novice, a "rookie," a seller to be taken advantage of. This can upset the balance of power at the sale. You should be in control and in charge. Your ignorance of the rules turns the control over to the more knowledgeable shopper.

If you do not play by the "rules," the buyers are less likely to play by the rules, resulting in, most significantly, less money in your pockets.

Shoppers are frustrated by changes in procedure.

When you announce a rule or practice that is contrary to "SOP," buyers are often put off and angry. They tend to be less inclined to purchase your goods then.

It is easier and more practical to follow the rules.

As with all rules, garage sale "SOP" is key in creating organization. It allows you to proceed without having to reinvent the wheel. (Think about it. You learned as a child that the flat, straight edges of a puzzle are its borders. How frustrated would you be if the next puzzle that you bought had the straight edges all in the middle? Would you buy puzzles from that manufacturer again? Why would you take the time to read all the inserts/literature when you have a workable frame of reference already?)

Sales run more smoothly if the rules are followed.

Following the rules makes the sale go more smoothly. Everyone is generally proceeding on the same basis, without wasting time on

Recognize the Rules

unnecessary explanations. (Again, think about it. You know that a green light means go and a red one means stop. This frame of reference works for you whether you are driving in New York or California, Texas or Maine.)

Garage sale rules create necessary structure.

Generally, rules develop because of their effectiveness. Rules provide a structure and system within which to work. It is wise to let the experience (and mistakes) of others (creating the basis of the rules) work to your advantage.

Garage sale "SOP" is protocol, and, as such, stands for doing things the right way.

Work smart - follow the rules.

Following the rules is part of working smart.

These are common, typical garage sale rules and protocol.

For an orderly, friendly and most profitable sale, pay attention to these typical, common rules:

1. The price of nearly all, if not all, items is negotiable.

2. There is little or no negotiation on a preview night or on an early bird look.

3. The sale will open 15 to 30 minutes before the listed start time.

4. If you open your garage and allow people to view your stuff (whether it is before or after the official hours of your sale), you

will also let them buy it. If your garage door is open while you are preparing for your sale, expect people to pop in, peer in, and ask if they can look and buy.

5.   All sales are paid by cash or check.

6.   All sales are cash and carry. Delivery is not provided.

7.   There are no refunds or exchanges, unless other arrangements are made. (Example: you might choose to tell someone to bring something back if it does not work.)

8.   Everything is purchased "as is," unless other arrangements are made.

No Refunds or Exchanges...

9.   There is no lying, deception, fraud or trickery. All sales and salesmanship is honest and above board.

Honesty is the best policy!

10.   The price of everything is easily ascertainable. The price can be found on the item or on a highly visible poster board.

11.   The price of everything is listed specifically, without reference to the seller's own, private labeling system.

12.   Items are not priced less than a nickel.

Recognize the Rules

No items are priced for a penny. Most items are priced in quarter increments.

13. The more a shopper buys, the better the deal you will give the buyer. This is known as a "volume discount."

14. There will not be a preview night unless it is a subdivision sale, and the neighborhood is participating in a preview.

15. Early birds will be tolerated, unless your ad says otherwise.

Is the sale open yet?

16. If you list rules in your ad, adhere to or abide by what you said. Specifically, if you say, "No early birds," it is against the rules to let early birds buy.

17. Garage sales are held during daylight hours, not at night. Exception: sometimes sales are held in the early evening when daylight is longest. Sellers have reported doing well during a 5:00 to 8:30 p.m. time slot, providing the garages were well lit. Be extra careful though, security wise.

Recognize the Rules

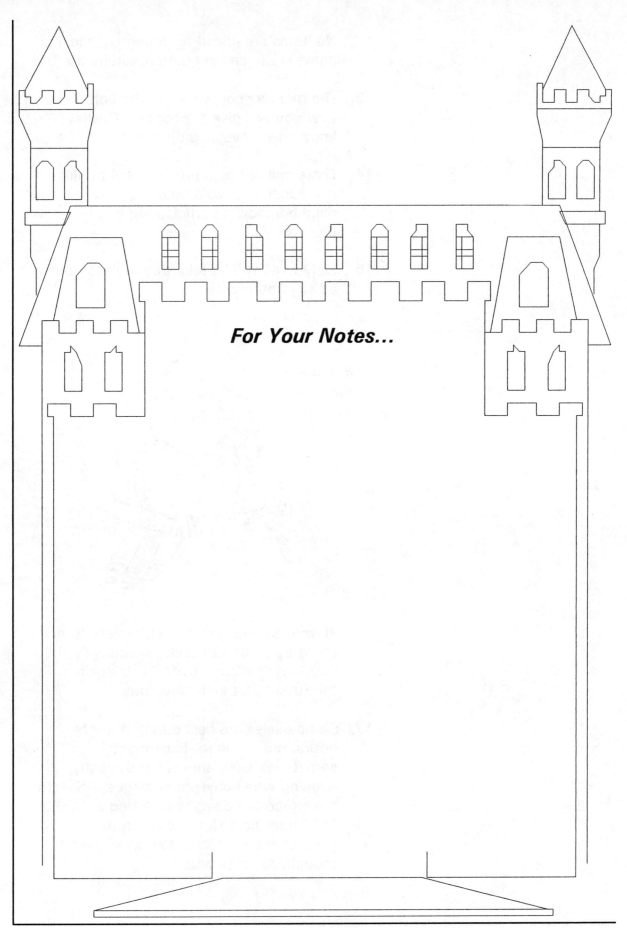

For Your Notes...

Recognize the Rules

S is for...

Staff your sale.

Arrange for extra helpers.

If at all possible, plan on having 2 or 3 helpers available on the morning(s) of your sale, that is, 30-45 minutes before the official starting/ opening time. These assistants can help you physically move your stuff from your garage to the driveway and front yard.   Remember that you want to attract as many people as possible to the sale, and one of the best ways to do that is to line your driveway with your belongings.

Direct your helpers with a minimum of personal involvement.

Tell your helpers what to do, how to help with a minimum of personal involvement on your part. (If you have to answer everyone's questions, you will not get your own jobs done and you will raise your own stress level unnecessarily.)

There are several very simple ways to do this.

Place things that have to be moved together.

Place everything that has to be moved outside of the garage in one location (such as underneath the tables, in front of the garage doors, the left corner of the garage, or the like) and tell your helpers to move that stuff outside.

Give a list of tasks to each helper.

Give a detailed list to each helper of what is to be moved. (Example: move all clothing racks to middle of driveway, place all boxes with pink bows in a row on the left side of the driveway, etc.) Be careful to be very specific and to label (such as with a bright sticker or bows) to serve as a double check.

Have more help during peak hours.

During the peak hours of the sale (the first 2 hours of the sale and the lunch hour), it is useful to have 1 to 2 helpers.

Assistants can do a number of things, all of which contribute to organization and efficiency. For example, your assistants can do the following:

❖ One person can bag the purchases, while you add.

❖ One person can add, while you take off the labels.

❖ One person can remove the hangers, while you collect the money.

❖ One person can collect the money, while you negotiate.

And so on...

At non-peak times, less assistance will be needed.

At other, non-peak, non-moving times, it is still worthwhile to have one aide, if possible. Your lone assistant is always a source of

Staff Your Sale

company and advice, giving you some security and conversation if needed. (Remember, part of your responsibility is to have fun!) Also, very often, it is helpful to have an assistant as a "go-for" person. Your "go-for" can get you some change, lunch, and whatever else you would like or need. Your "go-for" can also relieve you if you need to relieve yourself!

Check-out is easier with 2 people.

Check out will run more smoothly if there are two people working it. A suggested procedure uses one person to pull off tags/prices and separate by seller (by their initials) while the other person collects the money and bags the merchandise.

Extra help is handy at closing time.

At closing time, you will need 1 to 2 helpers as well. These assistants can help you return any unsold items to your garage for the next day(s) of your sale or for handling as a leftover.

It is helpful to have a helper with mechanical know-how.

If it is at all possible, one of your helpers should have some mechanical aptitude, or general knowledge of how your merchandise works. (This helper can tell a would-be buyer how a stroller closes, how a toy works, etc.) It is easier to sell stuff if the shopper knows how to use it.

Reward your helpers.

If your helpers do not have stuff at the sale, it's a very thoughtful idea to give your helper a little present to say "thanks" for the help, or to offer to work at her sale.

For your Notes...

Staff Your Sale

T is for...

Take note of the "Tools" of the garage sale trade.

There are tried and true "tools" for garage sales.

Masking tape is highly recommended.

Practically speaking, there are tried and true tools, well suited to the garage sale. This equipment (and a brief explanation of their usage) follows:

Masking tape: Primarily use to label your goods, putting prices and notes on the tape (including an identification of whose stuff it is, if you are having a multi-family sale) and then putting the masking tape on the item for sale. Masking tape is easily removed with little or no damage to the item itself. Masking tape stays stuck and does not come off by constant touching or handling, as other types of labels do. Masking tape may be used as well as a reinforcement to boxes, as a fastener to loose parts (such as keeping the extra buttons to a shirt, with the shirt), as a reminder pad (keep messages or unaccepted bids on a piece of masking tape and keep on your wall or on your fanny pack), and the like.

Tools of the Trade

Markers are handy.

Indelible/permanent marker: Use to label your goods. Apply to masking tape directly, with permanence, to label your merchandise or boxes. It will not run or bleed with water or hand touching. Black is easiest to read. Another color may be used to show a discount in price; you would re-write the new negotiated price over the original price in a different color. This easily shows you just how often and how much you negotiated for future garage sales.

A calculator is essential.

Calculator, preferably with a paper print-out: Use as an addition tool, plain and simple, to avoid the possibility of making a mistake in collecting money or giving change.

Display clothes on hangers.

Hangers: Use to hang your clothes on clothes racks. Keep your hangers when you make a sale, for use at your next sale.

Poster board has multiple uses.

Poster board: Use for signs (see below). Also can use as a tool to keep track of your sales.

When you sell an item, remove the masking tape label from the item. Place it on the poster board. Review every so often, especially after the sale, to see what sold and for how much. Start a new poster board or page on each day. Buyers on the second day may see a full board or page and assume the sale is picked over, with no good stuff left.

Tools of the Trade

Signs are key.

Signs: Use to advertise your sale and indicate that you are having a sale. Signs should be on either hot pink/ fuchsia, bright yellow, orange or chartreuse green heavy paper (poster board generally works) with black permanent marker writing. The bright colors are suggested to attract the attention of the passerby, who did not otherwise know about your sale, or to direct the driver who is heading to your house following your classified ad. Consider wrapping your signs in plastic wrap to protect against rain. You can make signs by stapling poster board to wooden stakes or by attaching poster board to a box. (See section below on stakes.) It is critical that any writing on the sign is legible. That means the writing must be neat, clear and large enough to be read at 30 mph. Your sign should state your address (either 200 Main Street) or a general location (Main and Second Street) or simply give directional arrows. (Make sure the arrows actually point to your house.) While directional signs are easy to follow, they might direct your buyer to another sale or may be taken by a less hard-working seller for their future sale. It is helpful to put the day and time of your sale on the sign.

Keep it simple!

Keep it simple though. People cannot read very much while driving at 30 miles per hour. Also, consider the same shaped signs to lead the driver to your street. Example: hearts, houses, diamonds, etc., anything to catch the eye. People do not appreciate it when they follow a sign and find out that the signs related to a sale held the weekend before.

The location of your signs is very important.

❖ Place your signs at as many nearby intersections as you can, depending on where you live. At a minimum, there should be a sign on your street and at every entry to your street or subdivision.

Tools of the Trade

Make sure that there are no laws, ordinances or rules preventing you from placing a sign at a particular location. Make sure you ask your neighbors if you may place a sign on their property. Check to make sure your signs are still up during the day. Be a good neighbor yourself and pick up your signs after your garage sale is over.

Make sure signs are firmly attached to wooden stakes.

Wooden stakes: Use in connection with your signs. Staple poster board to front of wooden stake. Staple poster board to back of wooden stake. Staple poster board signs together.

Hammer (regular carpenter's type and sledge type), stapler (staple gun and office type), duct tape, wire and nails: Use in connection with your signs, their installation and placement.

Banners/Flags/Balloons: Use in your front yard to identify that you are having a garage sale.

Clothing racks can display clothes to an advantage.

Clothing racks: Use to display your higher priced clothes. Note that clothing racks can be rented for a nominal cost. You can improvise with ladders, rope, garage door tracks, etc. (Often the garage door tracks will get grease on the hangers and run on other items, ruining them. Be careful.)

*Size indicators are a
nice touch.*

Size indicators or hoops for racks: Make a circle out of gift boxes to identify and separate sizes.

*Folding tables are
useful for breakables.*

Folding tables: Use to display your merchandise, especially breakables. Note that folding tables can be rented for a nominal cost and many of your neighbors will lend them to you, at no cost. Make sure your tables are sturdy and strong. (You don't want them to fall on anyone or anything.)

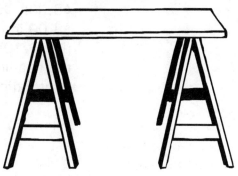

*Boxes are good for
many uses.*

Boxes: Use to store goods and display others. You will also need a box to put your hangers in after you make a sale, for the next sale.   If you are using a box in connection with your signs, make sure that you put the signs on all sides of the box. Make sure too that you put something heavy inside the box (such as a brick or telephone books) so that it does not blow over.

*Bags and sacks are
necessary for bagging
purchases.*

Bags/sacks: Use to package your buyers' purchases. You can save your own grocery bags or plastic sacks in preparation for the sale or you can purchase bags in bulk. Consider having a supply of bags with handles and offer to place the shoppers' holdings in the bag while he or she continues to shop. This can be done with other type of containers as well, such as a laundry basket.

*Newspapers are good
packing material.*

Newspapers: Use as packing material for breakables.

Tools of the Trade

Safety pins: Use to clip, pair or attach things together, especially relating to clothes. Pin matching socks to a pair of pants; pin a matching bow to a dress.

Garment "gun" and related supplies: If you decide to use this pricing method, (see chapter "Y,") you will need these supplies.

Have cash on hand to make change.

Cash : The suggested amount of cash on hand totals $70.00, equaling $16.00 in singles (16 x $1.00), $20.00 in five dollar bills (4 x $5.00), $30.00 in ten dollar bills (3 x $10.00), $3.00 in quarters (12 x $.25), $.50 in dimes (5 x $.10), $ .50 in nickels (10 x $.05).   See the heading, "C," "Carry Cash" for additional information.

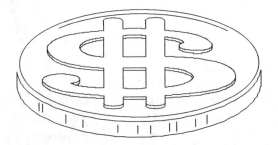

Fanny pack and/or cash box: Use to collect your money and to make change.

Make sure electical outlets are readily available.

Electrical Outlets and Batteries: Have available electrical outlets and batteries to prove that an item works. If an item does work, and you can prove it, you will get more money   for the item.

Identify the seller and helpers.

Badges or name tags: Use to identify the sellers and helpers. It is also a nice touch for

Tools of the Trade

sellers to wear a corresponding apron, or for all sellers to wear the same colors (e.g., green T-shirts and jeans).

Sheets will help neatness.

Sheets: Use, as needed, to lay on tables or over boxes so everything looks clean and neat.

Rope will separate not for sale items.

Rope: Use to separate areas of your own stuff.

Lightbulbs or lights: Have on hand to create extra light. Useful especially on a rainy, dark day.

There are optional tools as well.

There are optional, in a perfect world, items:

A dressing room could help increase sales.

Dressing room: In a perfect world, you would also be able to provide a dressing room of sorts for your patrons of clothes. If you have a room dividing frame or a makeshift one, use it in your garage. Otherwise, consider allowing your shoppers to use your bathroom. (Be careful here. Do this only if you have someone in your house to keep an eye on your valuables and on the bathroom and one or more people are outside at the sale.)

Shade for the sun might be helpful.

Umbrella: If you have one, you might consider using a table with an umbrella on it as your homebase during the sale. The umbrella will shield you from the elements (sun, especially)

Tools of the Trade

and enable you to be in the thick of the sale. Do not forget to mark the table and umbrella as "Not for sale."

A mirror is a good sales tool.

Mirror: Allows a shopper to see how he or she looks in an item.

Let the shopper measure.

Tape measure: Some buyers will fuss and fidget about the size of an item, not knowing if it will fit at their place. Sometimes this tool is helpful in making their purchase decision.

Add more tools for more participation.

Do not forget to increase the number of supplies you will need to accommodate and make room for the things that someone else may be bringing over to the sale. Ask everyone participating in the sale how much stuff they have to sell to make this assessment.

For your Notes...

Tools of the Trade

Supplies/Tools Checklist Practice Guide

ITEMS TO BUY *	NUMBER OF ITEMS	COST
Masking tape		
Permanent black marker		
Hangers		
Calculator		
Poster board		
Wooden stakes		
Hammer		
Stapler		
Banner/flags/balloons		
Size indicators		
Folding tables		
Boxes		
Bags/sacks		
Newspapers		
Cash		
Batteries		
Name tags		
Apron		
Sheets		
Rope/heavy string		
Room dividers		
Mirrors		
Tape measure		
Umbrella		
Sunscreen		
Cleaning supplies		
Safety pins		
Extra lightbulbs		
Electrical outlet/extension cord		
THINGS TO BORROW OR RENT	NUMBER OF ITEMS	COST
Clothes racks		
Folding tables		
Calculator		
Room dividers		
Hangers		
Hammer		
Wooden stakes		
Boxes		
Bags/sacks		
Extra lights		

* You may have many of these items on hand already.

U is for...

Use all your resources.

There are numerous resources available to help you make your garage sale a reality.

There is a steady supply of information, goods and services available to help you make your garage sale a reality (and a monetary success at that!)

There are numerous avenues to get information.

You can get information from friends, other sellers, and buyers.

Friends and neighbors who have had sales or who attend sales are an easy, readily available source of information.

Strangers may assist you with information as well. Do not hesitate asking others for knowledge while standing in line at a garage sale that you are visiting (perhaps before it opens) or while milling around at a sale.

You can get information from the seller at most sales. Try to make conversation (Examples: How is the sale going? Do you do this every year? Is it worth it?) "Fish" for more tidbits by paying compliments. (Examples: This is a really well organized sale, how did you do it?)

Check out ads.

Advertisements provide you with information, implicitly. See what catches your attention in

Use All Your Resources

an ad and why. Look for abbreviations used and make sure you know what they mean. You can figure out many garage sale rituals and rules simply by reading the ads.

See catalogues.

Catalogues (printed material) and verbal information from a store clerk or manager can assist with pricing, trends, top sellers, store layout, etc.

Make use of your own observations.

Capitalize on your own observations. Use these to your advantage.

Go to the library.

Library references are also available. There are few directly on point, or directly to the point. However, there are many good books on related topics such as retailing, negotiating, and marketing.

Get the supplies you need without an investment.

There are numerous ways to get the supplies you need, without making an investment in them.

Friends and neighbors may be willing to lend you tables or clothing racks.

Retailers, especially grocery stores, are likely to give you boxes or bags, at little or no cost.

Rental companies rent tables and chairs.

Rental companies rent tables, chairs and racks.

Private individuals also rent tables, chairs and racks. They often advertise in the garage sale section of the paper.

If you expect to have more sales, consider purchasing tables and racks.

If you expect to have sales regularly, consider buying tables or racks. Watch for liquidation sales of companies, where they are selling everything, including the fixtures.

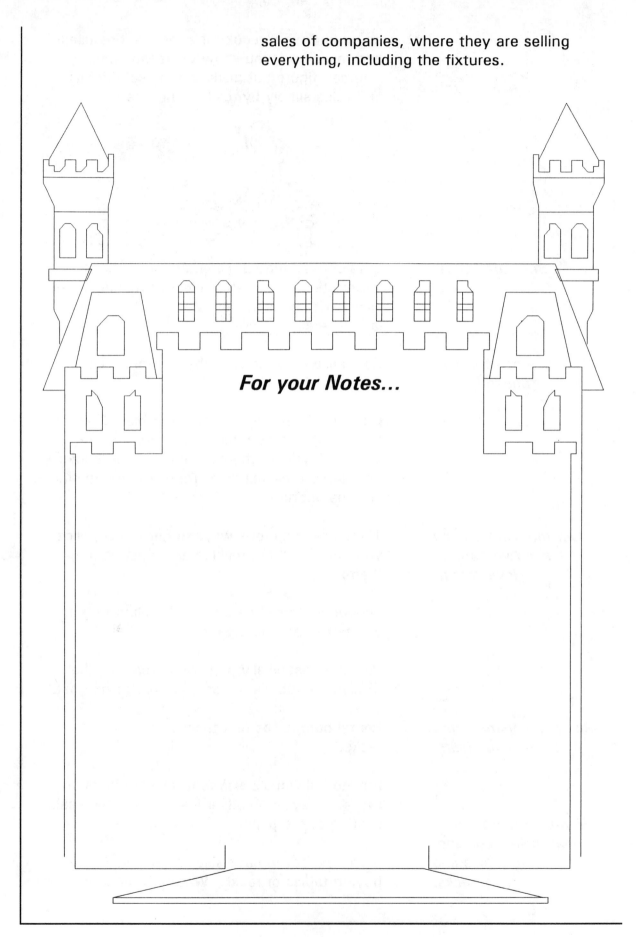

For your Notes...

Use All Your Resources

V is for...

View your sale from the customer's perspective.

Look at your sale from your customers' point of view.

Try to put yourself in the position of the customer at all times of the sale. This frame of reference and viewpoint should be behind your actions and decisions.

Ask yourself several questions.

Before you do anything related to your sale, ask yourself the following questions:

❖ "What will my buyer think?" (What would you think if you were in the buyer's position?)

❖ "What will my buyer say?" (What would you say if you were in the buyer's position?)

View Your Sale

❖ "How will my buyer feel?" (What would you feel if you were in the buyer's position?)

Concrete examples????

There are some concrete examples of how this works in practice:

Think about your buyer's ease of movement.

❖ When laying out your merchandise, think about your buyer's ease of movement.

❖ Can your buyer reach the item easily?

❖ Will your buyer be able to look at something while someone else is?

If you don't price something, the buyer will be intimidated.

If you do not price something, your buyer is going to have to ask you about it, at the risk of being intimidated or embarrassed. Isn't that how you would feel? Wouldn't you want to avoid that feeling? To be more customer friendly, price everything.

Price to negotiate.

If you refuse to negotiate and act like your prices are "too fair and reasonable" for any negotiating, aren't you making the buyer feel foolish and unreasonable? To be more customer friendly, price reasonably and price to negotiate. Be prepared to negotiate on everything, even if it is just a little.

Make your buyer feel wanted...

Be more customer-friendly. Make your sale a good experience for the buyer.

If you have signs all over with disclaimers and rules (such as No refunds or exchanges; Not responsible for accidents; etc.), your buyer is likely to feel unwanted, insulted and child-like. Wouldn't you? Get rid of the signs to be more customer friendly.

Try to make coming to your sale and buying from your sale, a good experience from the customer's point of view. (See also "H," "Hospitality.")

For your Notes...

View Your Sale

137

W is for...

Wonder not When to have a garage sale.

The timing of your sale affects earning potential.

The timing of your sale can and often does affect the amount of money you will make at the sale. The expression, "timing is everything," is truer than the garage sale seller might expect or realize.

Figure out the best time to hold your sale.

Timing questions fall in several different categories: what time of year to have the sale; what time of month to have the sale; what day(s) of the week to have the sale; and what times of the day to have the sale.

Time of the year:

The best time of the year to hold a sale is...

Have your sale when most people want to be outdoors. People tend to take Sunday-type drives or leisurely walks during nice weather and are more likely to take the time to enjoy your sale while enjoying the weather.

"Clear and sunny on Wednesday..."

Probably avoid mid-summer or mid-winter.

Have your sale when the weather outdoors is tolerable. It should not be oppressively hot or cold; it should not be held during a rainy or snowy season.

Depending on your geographical location and its climate, you probably will not have a sale in the middle of the winter or in the middle of the summer. Spring, early summer and early fall are generally the preferred seasons or times of the year for garage sales.

Generally April, May and June are popular months.

❖   In the majority of the United States, garage sales are most popular in April, May, June and September.

❖   Do not have a sale around a holiday. Too many people are unavailable to buy; they are either out-of-town or busy with holiday-related plans.

4th of July

Don't plan your sale during a major event, sporting or otherwise.

❖   Do not have a sale around a major national or local event, such as the Super Bowl, a county bazaar, etc., if the majority of shoppers will be attending or watching it, and not out at garage sales.

Avoid income tax payment time.

Take advantage of any event or circumstance which makes a potential shopper cash-rich. Examples: known corporate/company bonus time; IRS refunds, etc.

On the other hand, avoid any time of the year that makes a potential shopper cash-poor. Examples: After Christmas; tax time; etc.

Time of the month:

The best time of month is.....

Consider holding your sale around the first or fifteenth of the month. Many people get paid on these days and are therefore more likely to have the needed (or extra!) cash to buy your merchandise.

Avoid holidays.

Avoid having a sale around a holiday. Too many people are unavailable to buy; they are either out-of-town or busy with holiday-related plans.

Take advantage of any event or circumstance which would attract buyers. If you live near a school, consider having your sale when a school event takes place; if you live on the way to the fairground, consider having your sale when the fair is held; etc.

The best day of the week is....

Day of the week:

As you have learned from many of the letters

of the "garage sale alphabet," it is important to follow the cues of others when establishing your own garage sale. This is especially true when deciding which day of the week to have your sale.

The best days vary by region.

There are significant regional or geographical differences as to the days a sale are held. For example, in one location, 99% of the sales are held from Wednesday through Saturday; in another place, sales are mostly held on Fridays through Mondays. Your sale will not likely be successful if you have it on a Monday in the first region, and would be most profitable in the other.

You need to do some research and see what is the norm in your area. (See especially letters "A," "E" and "I"). Have your sale during the most popular days of the week in your area.

Consider having your sale on all of the best days.

If you have the time, energy and patience, have the sale during *all* of the most popular days, even if that numbers as many as four days. You will have the greatest opportunity (literally) to sell your merchandise. It will also afford you the luxury of quickly reacting, on a more paced rate. (See letter "Q.")

Include at least one weekend day in your sale schedule.

If you do not have the time, energy or patience to last that long, have the sale on at least one weekday day and one weekend day. These days should be back to back. This combination will enable those people who work, and those people

Wonder Not When to Have Your Sale

141

who do not, to attend your sale.

If you can only have your sale on one day, have it on a weekend day. This way both working and non-working people can attend. Especially if you advertise the sale as a "One day only event," non-working people, who would be inclined to go to sales on less crowded days, are still very likely to come to your sale.

The best time of day is....

Time of the day:

Have your sale only during hours of day light. This generally means holding a sale anytime between 7:30 a.m. or 8:00 a.m. and 4:30 or 5:00 p.m., depending on your time zone and time of year. This strategy is safer for you and the customers. Additionally, and more practically, it is very hard to view merchandise in the dark, even with your garage lights on.

Some people prefer to have shorter sale hours.

Many people recommend fewer hours for the sale, and suggest closing between noon and 2:00 p.m. It really is a personal choice depending on your own goals and objectives (see letter "Z" especially). Recognize this though: the later it gets at the sale, the less negotiating power you generally will have. In fact, some seasoned shoppers venture out after noon only, on purpose, hoping to get a fabulous buy on something that was too high priced for morning shoppers.

If you have to hold a sale at a less than ideal time...

If you must have a sale at a less than perfect time of the year, month or day, you will need to work a bit harder and a bit smarter.

You will have to walk up hill, and swim up stream, so to speak, to get people to your sale. For example, you will need to place your ad in more places; you will need to make your ad longer and more mouth-watering; you will need to use more untraditional ways to tell people about your sale.

You will also have to compensate for whatever makes your sale date a less than ideal one.   For example, if you want to have your sale in the winter, you may need to have your sale inside or in a heated garage and advertise this warmth.

You may have other alternatives as well. You may wish to investigate renting a booth at a flea market, or selling your big items by classified ad, or consigning before a sale, or asking a friend or neighbor if they will store and later sell your stuff for a commission.

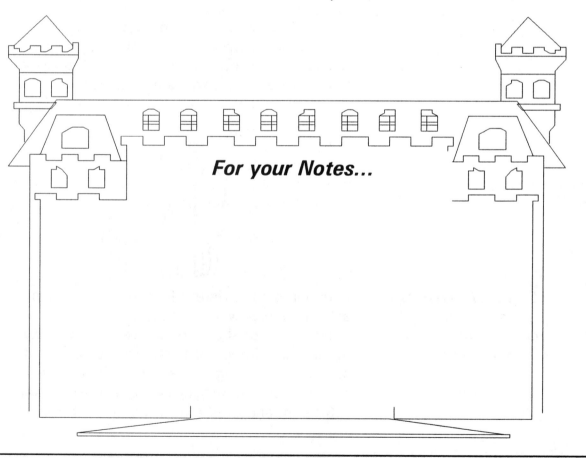

For your Notes...

Wonder Not When to Have Your Sale

X is for...

Expect these expectations.

You can expect certain things to happen at your sale.

Some occurrences and experiences are a probability, perhaps even a certainty, at a garage sale. If you know what to expect, you can plan accordingly.

Expect "early birds."

Expect "early birds" at your sale. (Early birds are shoppers who arrive at your sale **long** before it officially opens.) Early birds want a jump on your sale; they want to be the first to look at and buy anything of interest to them. Early birds will approach your house hours, even days, before your sale is scheduled to begin. Early birds are often dealers and re-salers (people who buy stuff at garage sales cheaply and sell them again, often after fixing them up, removing stains or the like).

Expect shoppers to arrive 15 to 30 minutes before your scheduled time.

Early birds are different from prompt garage sale shoppers (who tend to be regulars). Expect prompt shoppers and regulars to arrive at your sale fifteen to thirty minutes before its scheduled opening. (Example: if your sale is set for 8:00 a.m., regulars will arrive between 7:30 a.m. and 8:00 a.m.). Some of these

Expect These Expectations

Some sellers allow people to shop before opening time.

shoppers will line up outside for your sale, politely waiting on the driveway or in their cars for you to open your doors. Others are much more aggressive; they will knock on your doors and act insulted by your failure to start the sale until starting time.

As stated in "R," Recognize Rules, most sellers allow people to shop and buy before the sale starts, as long as it does not hinder set-up or organization, or otherwise interfere with your plans.

Any time your garage door is open, and garage sale merchandise is in it, expect people to stop and buy.

If it's a neighborhood sale, expect neighbors to preview the night before.

If you are participating in a neighborhood or subdivision sale, expect people to come to your sale the night before it opens. This is called "previewing." It is an attempt by sponsoring home owners' associations to give non-participating neighbors first chance to buy their neighbors' goods. Where subdivision sales are common, it is equally common for there to be a preview night and for it to be "crashed" (accepted and anticipated) by non-neighbors.

Expect busy and slow times.

Expect there to be slow times at your sale and busy times as well. The first thing in the morning will be the busiest time. Mid-afternoon will be your slowest time. Expect too to make more money on the first day of your sale.

Expect to make less money each day of the sale.

On the second day of your sale, expect to make 1/2 as much money as you did on the first day. On the third day of your sale,

Expect These Expectations

expect to make 1/4 as much money as the first day.

Expect to spend some money to make money.	Expect to spend money to make money. You will need to buy materials, run an ad, and the like. Also, most sellers wind up buying lunch and/or dinner out during the sale (pizza is most common) since their time is at a premium then.
Expect to bargain.	Expect to negotiate. (Review letter, "B.")
Expect to work hard.	Expect to work hard, in preparation for the sale, during the sale itself and in wrapping it up.
Expect touching.	Expect kids to touch all the merchandise within their reach, especially the toys.
	Expect your display to look like a tornado went through it, within 2 to 2 1/2 hours after your sale begins . Many shoppers will paw through your stuff, and will not put things back where they belong. Expect to straighten up your merchandise several times a day for each day of your sale.
Expect to have "leftovers."	Expect to have "leftovers." (Review letter "L" for dealing with this.)
Expect to earn between $100.00 and $2,500.00 per sale.	Expect to earn between $100.00 and $2,500.00 per sale. This range is admittedly a large one, as earnings are very much based on your individual circumstances. Your gross proceeds will largely depend on the quantity and quality of your merchandise, the length of your sale and timing issues, as well as your ability and willingness to negotiate and react.

Expect These Expectations

For your Notes...

Expect These Expectations

Y is for...

Yard Sale with Others, or, Yours, mine and ours:

decide about multi-family and neighborhood sales...

Decide whether or not to participate in a multi-family, neighborhood or subdivision sale.

A multi-family sale is encouraged.

There are many sound reasons to have a multi-family sale. Assuming that you can work out details and procedures for having a sale with your friends and neighbors (see exceptions and warnings below), a multi-family sale is strongly encouraged.

The more stuff you have to sell, the more you can earn.

The more stuff that you have at your sale, the more money that you can make, and the more profits which can and will be generated at your sale. If you are not sure that you have

Yard Sale with Others

enough inventory, you should consider having a multi-family sale.

How do you know if you have enough merchandise for sale?

How do you know if you have enough stuff for a sale? There are several ways to guesstimate this. You have enough of your own stuff if:

❖ You have 50 or more items for sale; or

❖ If you get your asking price on one half of your available merchandise, you will clear at least 10 to 20 times your costs in having the sale (e.g., advertising, tools, supplies, etc.); or

❖ On an hourly basis, you will earn the equivalent of at least $5.00 an hour; or

❖ You can fill up two large folding tables or four card tables with merchandise; or

❖ Without counting, measuring or laying out your stuff, your "eyeballs" and "gut" tell you that you have enough to sell.

Having friends and neighbors participate can work to your advantage.

Even if you have enough of your own merchandise, having your friends and neighbors participate with you can work to your advantage.

There is good will.

Having a multi-family sale can bring you good will. If your neighbors' items are for sale at your house, your neighbors are less likely to object to all the additional neighborhood traffic associated with the sale; they are less likely to gripe about any inconvenience associated with

Yard Sale with Others

149

a sale.

There are additional supplies.

Having a multi-family sale usually brings you additional tools and supplies. Your friends and neighbors tend to be very willing to lend you a table or rack when there is something in it for them. When you sell their stuff, there is something very tangible and real in it for them.

> Do not forget to increase the number of supplies you will need to accommodate and make room for the things that someone else may be bringing over to the sale. Ask everyone participating in the sale how much stuff they have to sell.

There is additional help.

Having a multi-family sale usually brings you additional staff. If you are selling your friends and neighbors' stuff, they will be probably be more likely to help you at the sale itself.

Your friends and neighbors should offer to pay for the sale.

If your friends and neighbors participate with you in the sale, they can (and should offer to) share in the expenses of having a sale. This will, in turn, increase your profits; since "revenue minus expenses equals profit," once you reduce your expenses, your profits will automatically increase.

More people means more stuff.

If your friends and neighbors have unique, unusual or in demand merchandise, your sale will be advantaged. People tend to buy more than one item (statistically your stuff), even if they come to the sale in search of that one thing that your neighbor brought over to sell.

Set some guidelines for multi-family sales.

> **Warning for multi-family sales: Be careful to set some guidelines with your participating friends and neighbors if you are going to have a multi-family sale.**

Yard Sale with Others

Understand and agree on your negotiating power for and on others' stuff. Since negotiating and bargaining is key in a garage sale, do not undermine yourself by not having negotiating power for others.

Everyone should have their own labels.

Make sure that each participant labels their own stuff. Label or identify each item with the participant's initials (ex: M for Mary, K for Karen, L for Linda, etc.) If more than one participant has the same initial (L for Lisa and Linda), then use their last initial alone, or use it with their first initial.

Keep track of everyone's sales.

Keep track of everyone's sales. There are a couple of simple ways to keep track of each participant's sales.

Use separate posterboard or notebooks.

You can use a notebook with a separate page for each seller-participant, or you can use a separate piece of posterboard for each seller. Put the price tags (the removed masking tape or color coded dots) on each person's page or board to show what that seller sold.

Use different dots.

Use different color tape or markers or paper (attached to the item by straight pins or safety pins or staples, depending on the item for sale) when marking the price. This works especially well when you use colored dots. For example: All green dots or markings belong to Valerie, all pink dots or markings belong to Judy, all yellow dots or markings to Paula.

Judy = $125.00
Sam = $315.50
Terry = $55.75
Lisa = $553.50
and so on......
....

Yard Sale with Others

Separate with bags.

We recently learned of another clever way. The sellers labeled their items with a price tag, made of sturdy paper, which was perforated at the bottom. The tags, purchased at an office supply kind of store, come in different colors. Each seller had a different color tag and each seller individually marked their tag. (These kind of tags require you to mark a price on the top half of the tag and on the bottom half of the tag. To some, this seems like double work. These tags are usually attached to the item with a garment "gun," requiring purchase of other, less traditional materials.) When an item sold, the cashier tore off the bottom half of the tag and put that tag in a plastic bag. Each seller had a different color tag and therefore a different plastic, locking type, of bag for their sales. This eliminated basically any accounting at the check out stand; rather each seller could add up his or her little paper tags and total up what was in the plastic sealed bags only at the end of the sale.

Keep the bookkeeping simple.

There are endless possibilities here. Do whatever works for you and your garage sale colleagues. By all means, try to keep it simple. Try to limit the amount of writing you have to do at the sale itself...hopefully there will be too much selling for such accounting.

Oops, here is a shortage.

Do not lose your friends over accounting issues. Agree what will happen if there is a shortage or overage of money, that is, if the books do not reconcile.

Yard Sale with Others

Have a pricing party.

Consider having a "pricing party." Invite all the people who are selling stuff at your sale to come over and price together as a group. You can have prizes, games and a lot of fun or you can make it very business-like. Your choice!

Be consistent with prices.

Compare and contrast the prices set by the friends or neighbors participating in the sale, and make sure that they are similar. This is critical. (Ex: If Alice is selling towels for $1.00 each, Debby cannot sell towels for $2.50 a piece.) Re-set the prices to be the same (at whatever price the parties agree to), or set forth the difference in prices (ex: towels with lace, towels of pima cotton, etc.).

The buyer should not be negatively affected by a multi-family sale.

If you are having a multi-family garage sale, try not to let that fact become painful or difficult for your shoppers. Having a multi-family sale is supposed to attract buyers and encourage purchases, not the opposite. For example: Do not make the buyer pay for all "red dot" purchases over here and all "green dot" purchases over there; do not refuse to bargain on an item because "it is not mine;" etc.

Some sellers take a percentage of the total sales.

Some sellers take a percentage (one to ten percent) of their neighbors' sales proceeds for selling their stuff. Consider this very carefully; it may change your relationship with your friends as well as transform the non-commercial nature of your garage sale.

A multi-family sale is not the same as a neighborhood sale.

A multi-family sale is not the same as a neighborhood sale. A multi-family sale is held at one person's house; two or more families

Yard Sale with Others

bring their stuff to one central location for sale. A neighborhood sale is held within a neighborhood or subdivision at separate homes; the participants are not necessarily sharing anything other than the day of the sale.

Participate in a neighborhood sale if...

There are some issues to think about before participating in a neighborhood sale.

Neighborhood sales are great for first time sellers.

Neighborhood garage sales are often an ideal starting point for a first time garage sale seller.

The risk is very limited.

The risk to the seller is very limited in terms of both effort and expense. Specifically, advertising costs are minimal. Usually the whole neighborhood splits the cost of the ads, costing as little as a dollar to participate and you do not have to make up your own sign. Generally a committee plans and markets the event and you just show up at your own house with your stuff.

If you choose to not have a sale, just don't open your garage door.

If you choose not to participate at the last minute for whatever reason, you just do not open your garage door.

If you get tired of the sale, you just close up; if you are unsure of yourself on any sale-related issue, you can follow the lead of your neighbors, many of whom may be more experienced than you are at garage selling.

People flock to subdivision sales.

People gravitate, flock and rush to subdivision sales. The number of attendees is greater than most sellers could expect if they hold their own, separate sales. Stated most simply, if you open your garage during a neighborhood sale, you will be greeted (and probably flooded) with shoppers. You do not need to have a lot of merchandise, given the traffic in the subdivision.

However, there is more competition.

However, there is an important flipside to this happy scenario. With so many places to

Yard Sale with Others

shop, so much different merchandise to look at within the particular neighborhood, you are apt to see a fussier buyer, one who senses, suspects, and/or is willing to gamble that there is a better deal at the next house or the one after that. In sum, there is just too much competition.

If you are pricing on the high side, and you have enough of your own inventory, you should consider carefully participating in the subdivision sale.

There is a compromise.

An interesting compromise might be struck, one which is highly recommended. Participate in the subdivision sale and hold your sale on one other day (preferably consecutive) when the subdivision is not having a sale. (Example: subdivision is having its sale on Friday and Saturday. Have yours on Thursday, Friday and Saturday.) Moreover, advertise your own sale independently, as if you were not a part of the neighborhood extravaganza. This will attract those shoppers who are looking for the merchandise you have to sell, rather than those who are just browsing.

Where should the sale be held?

As a real estate agent will tell you, no doubt, when dealing with real estate and sales, the key is location, location and location.

The ideal location is....

The ideal location for a garage sale is a house on a busy street or very, very close to a busy street. This will give you the most exposure and attract lots of passerbys in addition to those flocking to your sale because of your ads. This ideal location should have lots of parking too, and a large, uncluttered "garage" space for your stuff to be showcased in at a sale. A spacious driveway is also welcomed, so you can line it with your goods.

The worst location is....

The worst location is one which is very difficult to find, off the beaten path, so to speak, with hardly any traffic except for the traffic otherwise going to your house or to your friends or neighbors' homes.

Few locations are perfect and few are horrible; most will do just fine.

If you have less than an ideal location...

If you have less than an ideal location for a garage sale, you have several options:

1. Have your sale at the house of a friend or relative who has a better location.

2. Have your sale with several of your neighbors, increasing the likelihood that people will come to your location.

3. Have your sale at your house anyway, but step up the amount of advertising and marketing about the sale.

4. Make the possibilities at your sale so mouth-watering that any garage sale shopper would be "a fool" to miss it.

Yard Sale with Others

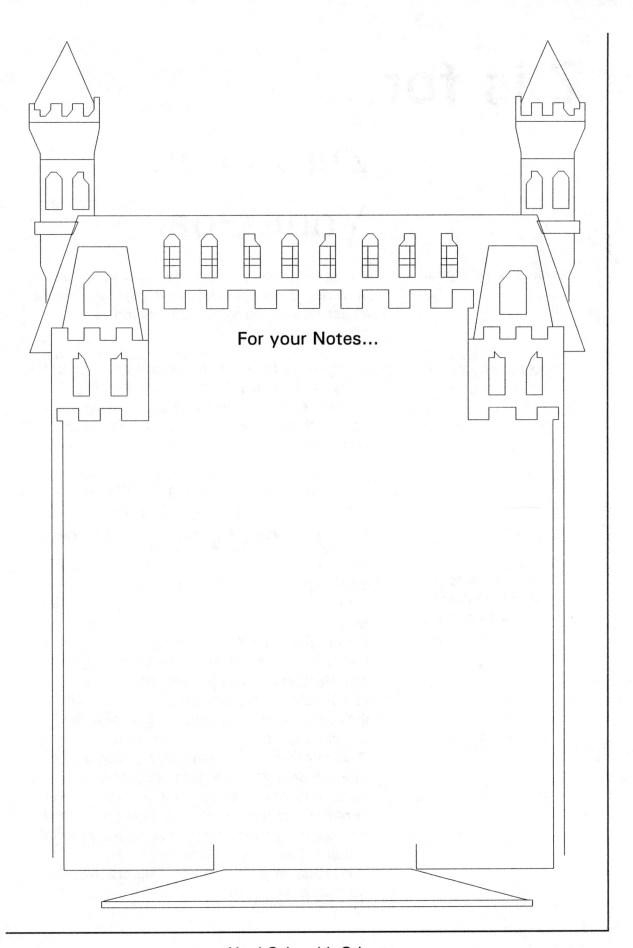

For your Notes...

Yard Sale with Others

Z is for...

Zero in on Your Goal

Identify your goal.

It is critical that you identify what your goal is in having a garage sale. Your goal will impact all aspects of the sale, from pricing to advertising to marketing.

Use the strategy to match your goal.

Most sellers have a combination or range of goals. It is typical for a seller to be very "proud" of some items and equally carefree about others. Use the strategy best suited to your goals.

Work Toward Your Goal...

If your goal is to get rid of your "junk," price and sell accordingly.

If your goal is "to get rid of your junk," you are interested in maximizing your profit as long as it will reduce your inventory. Translation: before giving your stuff away, you are going to see if you can make any money on your merchandise. If you are this kind of seller, you should mark your items to sell, despite their worth or value, despite their cost, and despite any financial or emotional cost to you. (This generally means that everything at the sale will cost $1.00 or less, in quarter increments.) Remember that you do not want to re-pack or re-store the merchandise after the sale, so your prices should be very flexible and you should not refuse any offer, unreasonable as it may be. You probably want to post a sign alerting buyers to your

Zero In On Your Goal

willingness to deal, although astute shoppers will probably figure it out anyway.

Recommended compromise...

> You can acccomplish your goal of "getting rid of your junk" without giving away your stuff. (After all, that is what this information is all about in the first place!) In a nutshell, if you recognize what has value at a sale and what does not; if you divorce yourself from any sentimental value an item may have; and if you play by the rules of the "garage sale game," you should be able to meet your goal quite nicely with personal financial gain.

If you want to regain some of what you originally paid, educate the buyer.

If your goal is to recoup as much as possible of the retail price which you paid, your pride in the merchandise should be seen at the sale. Your aim will be to educate the buyers of the value of a purchase, and to emphasize the quality of the merchandise. You should be prepared to consign any unsold items and explain this to the shopper.

> Note: If you are planning on consigning your garage sale items, make sure that your garage sale price is, in fact, what you would get at a consignment store. (If the consignor is going to pay you $4.00 for the shirt at its sale, why mark it $6.00 now?) Make sure that there is a good consignment store willing to accept your item or type of goods. (Is there an outlet for used mens' clothing? shoes? used furniture? etc.?) Make sure that your goods are otherwise eligible for consigning. (Are they clean? pressed? in perfect condition? etc.?)

Garage sales are great ways to recycle things you no longer want.

Try to think of having a garage sale as a form of recycling. No matter what the outcome, you are doing something which is not only to your economic advantage, but is ecologically, environmentally smart, to the world. (Talk about having a global outlook!)

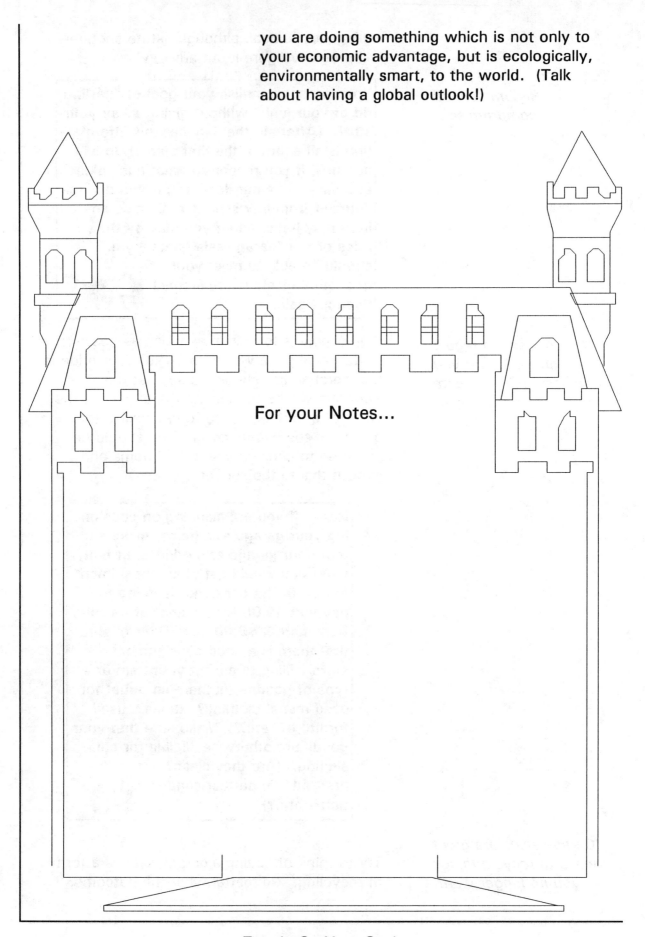

For your Notes...

Zero In On Your Goal

A Final Word

You did it!

You did it! You turned the fairy tale into reality and made more money at your sale than you would have predicted originally.

Ask yourself these questions:

What did you learn?

What was most helpful to you in real garage sale life?

What surprised you the most?

What would you tell your friends if they ask about your experience?

Will you do it again?

What, if anything, will you do differently?

Have you become a garage sale fanatic? Lover? Devotee? Or a despiser?

We are interested in your feedback.

We, garage sale gurus, those who love any and all garage sales, are very interested in your opinion and feedback. In fact, the publisher is prepared to offer you a discount on any future publications or books about garage sales if you will fill us in on all the gory details.

Fill us in on your garage sale experiences.

And, if you were already a garage sale lover, or have become one based on (or in spite of?) your experience, let us know if you would be interested in fostering a network of garage sale lovers, such as with a newsletter or the like.

Let us hear from you.

We look forward to hearing from you in the future and are glad to have played a part in your garage sale success!

Our address is:

Clover Creations
P.O. Box 26422
Mail Stop J25
Shawnee Mission, KS 66225

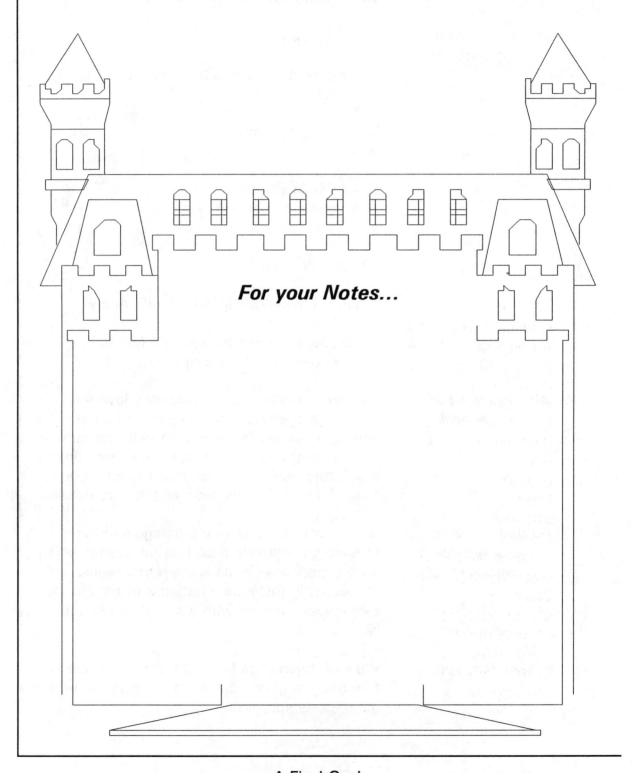

For your Notes...

A Final Goal

Index

Index

continued...

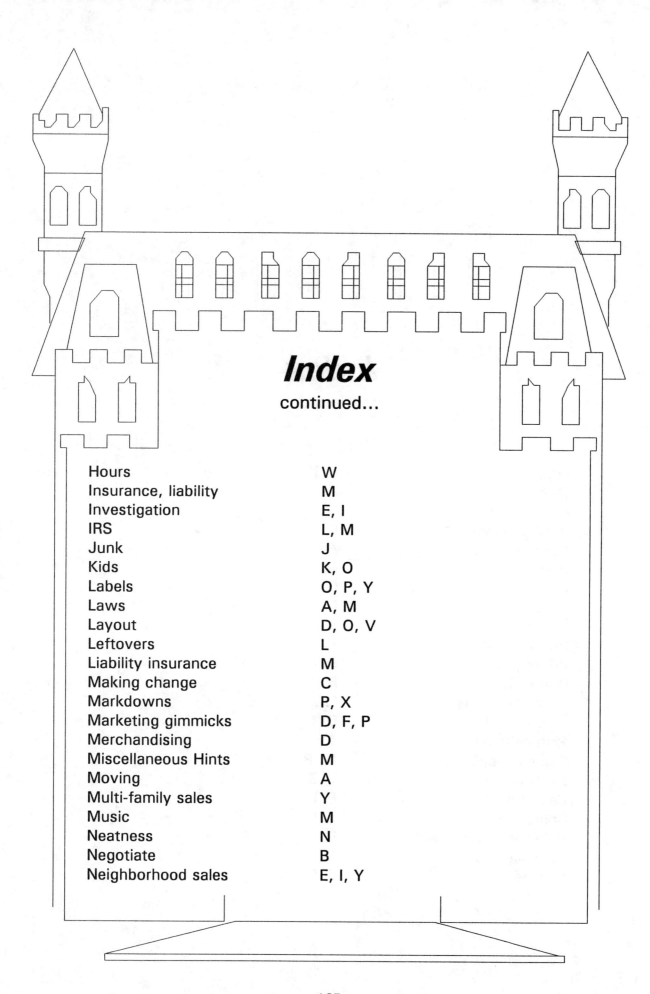

Index

continued...

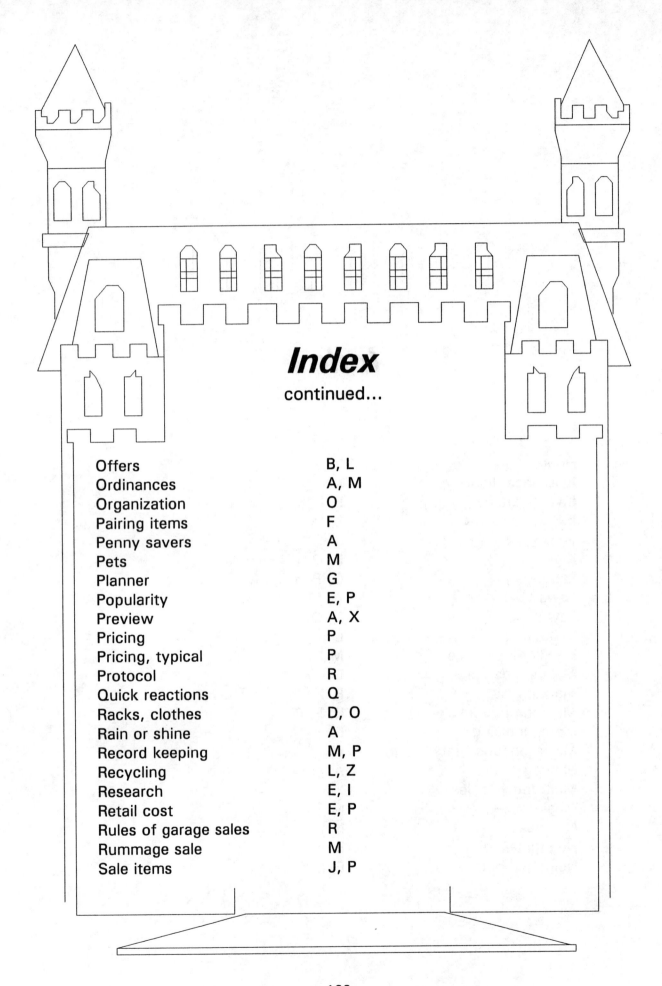

Index

continued...

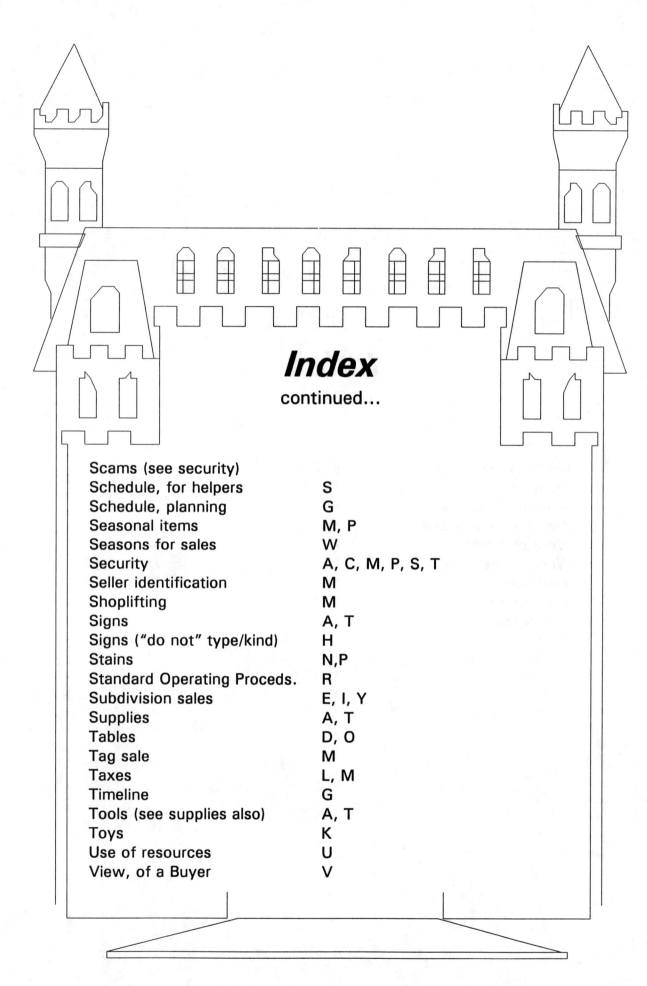

Index

continued...

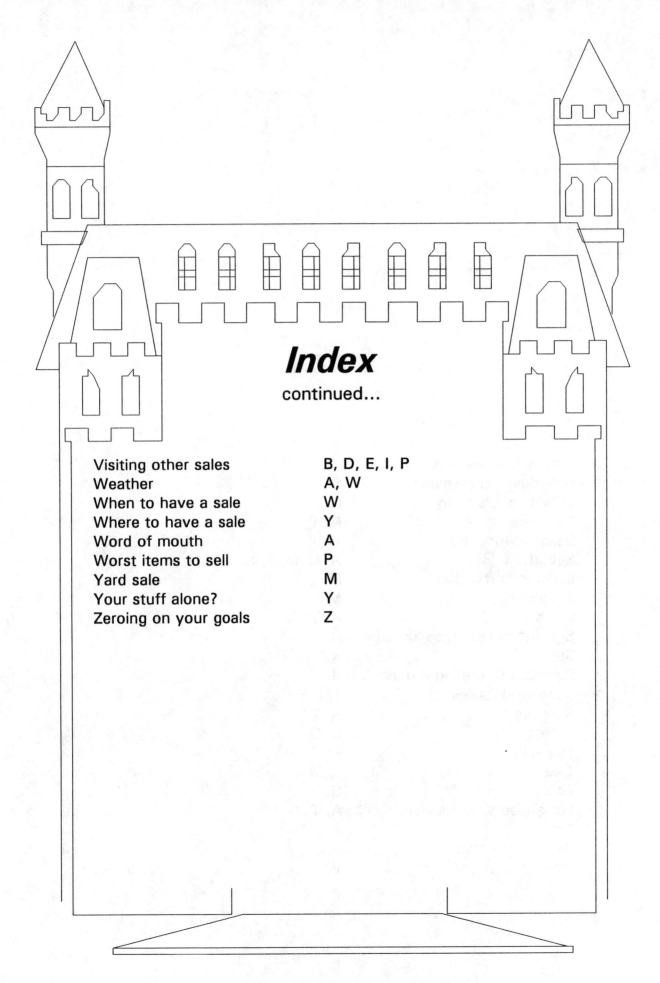

Index

continued...

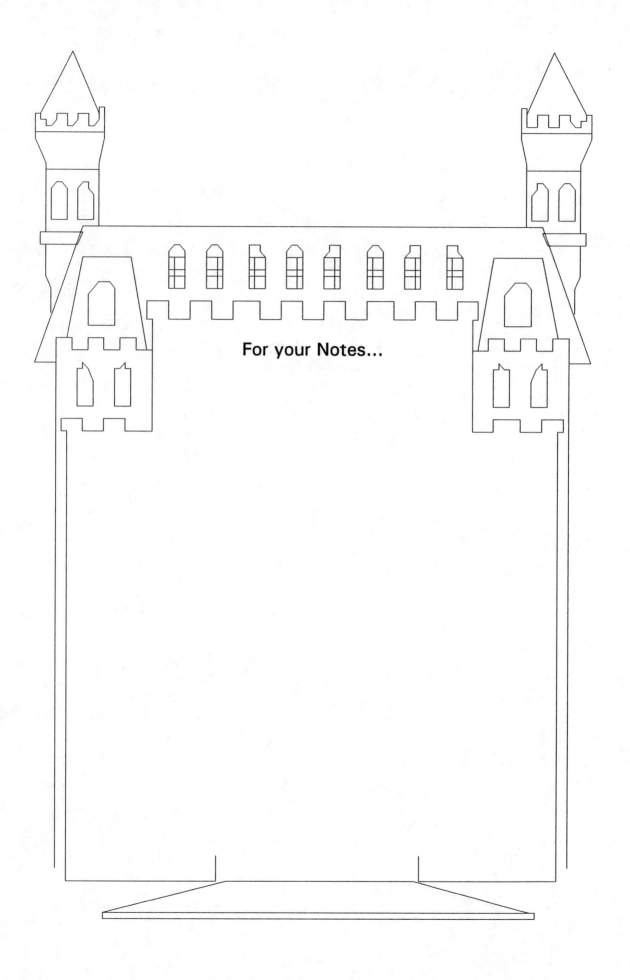

For your Notes...

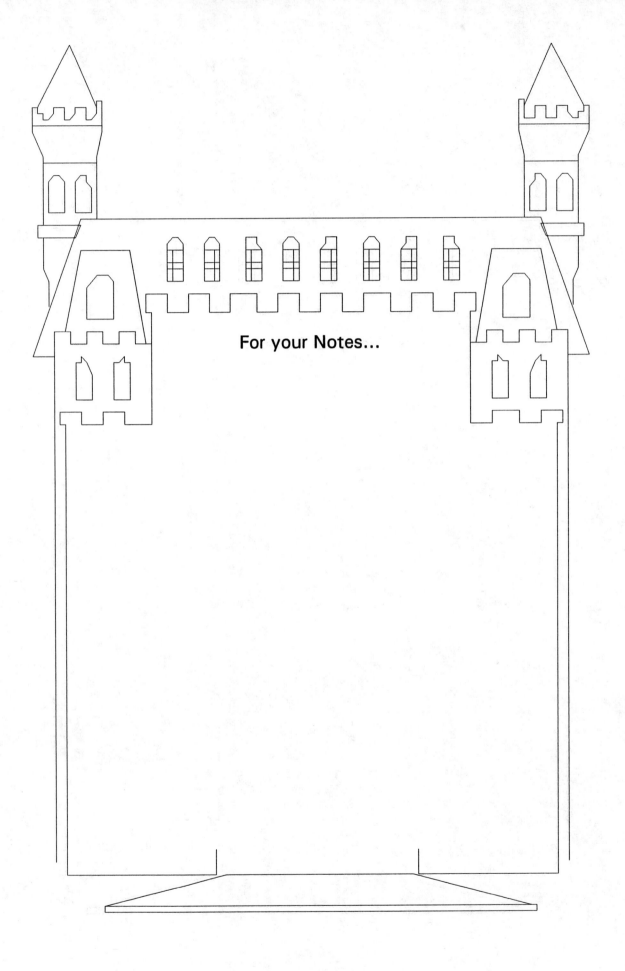

For your Notes...

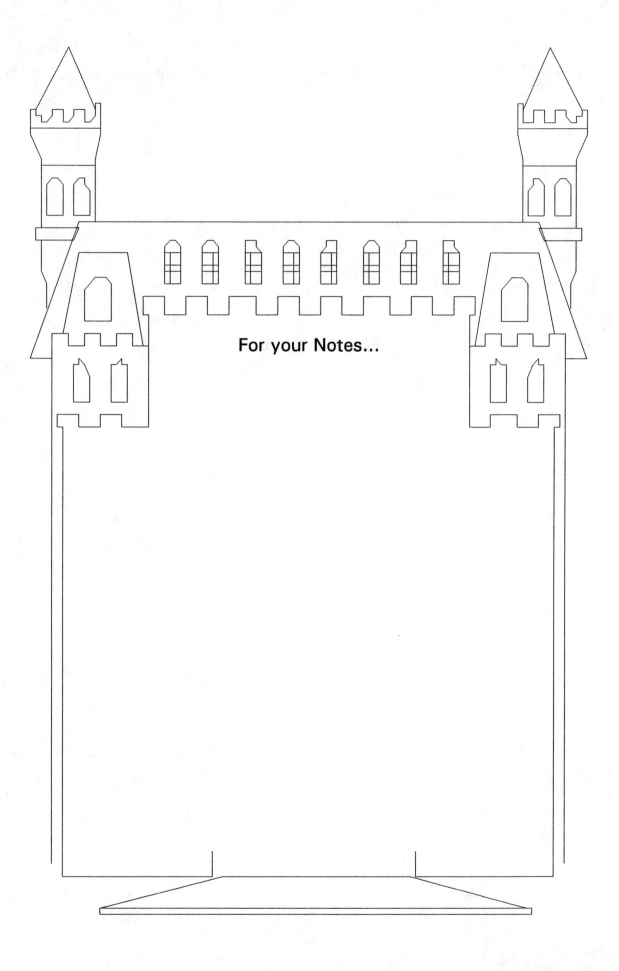

For your Notes...

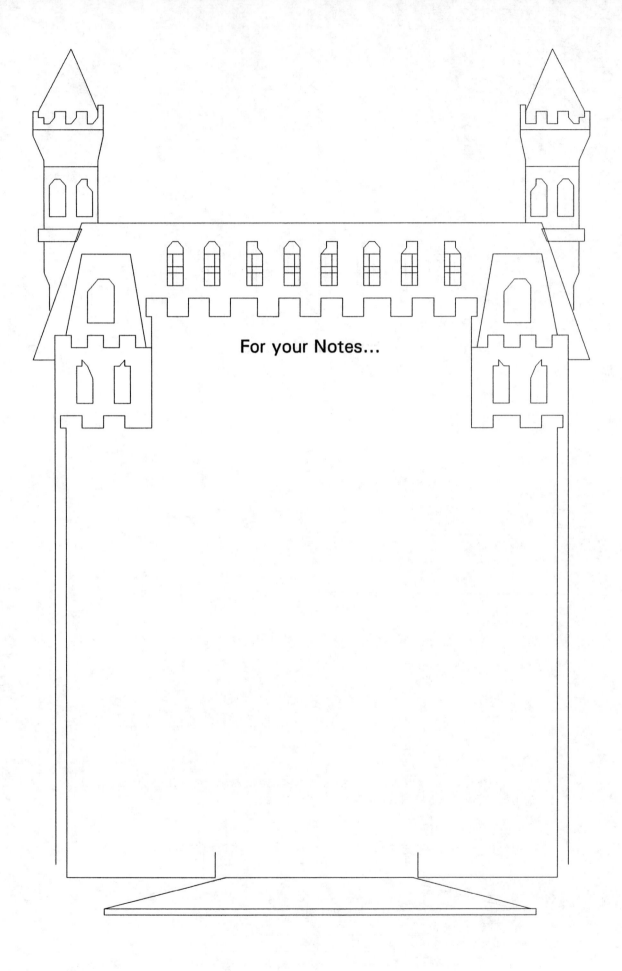

For your Notes...

Order Blank

Telephone orders: Call Toll Free: 1-(888)-5 A.M. SALE (1-888-526-7253).
Please have your Visa or MasterCard ready.

Fax orders: (913) 851-2558

Postal Orders: Clover Creations, P.O. Box 26422, Mail Stop J25,
                Shawnee Mission, KS 66225

Please send _____ (number) of copies of "Once Upon A Garage Sale...

My
Name:_____

My shipping address: _____
                                        Street

                      _____
                      City   State   Zip Code

My telephone number: (   )_____

Sales Tax:
Please add 6.875% for books shipped to Kansas addresses. (That amounts to
$1.03 for each book purchased at $14.95)

Shipping and Handling:
Please add $4.00 for the first book and $2.50 for each additional book.

Payment:
Check ____
Credit card: Visa ____   MasterCard ____
        Card number: _____
        Name on card: _____

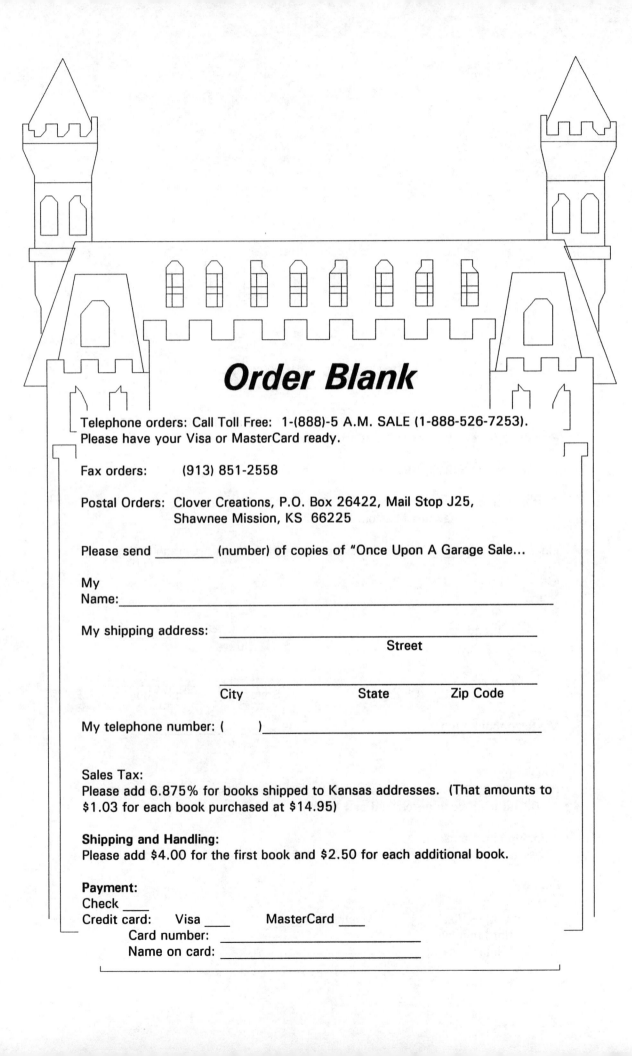

Order Blank

Telephone orders: Call Toll Free: 1-(888)-5 A.M. SALE (1-888-526-7253).
Please have your Visa or MasterCard ready.

Fax orders: (913) 851-2558

Postal Orders: Clover Creations, P.O. Box 26422, Mail Stop J25,
                Shawnee Mission, KS 66225

Please send _____ (number) of copies of "Once Upon A Garage Sale...

My
Name:_____

My shipping address: _____
                                                    Street

                      _____
                      City   State   Zip Code

My telephone number: (   ) _____

Sales Tax:
Please add 6.875% for books shipped to Kansas addresses. (That amounts to
$1.03 for each book purchased at $14.95)

Shipping and Handling:
Please add $4.00 for the first book and $2.50 for each additional book.

Payment:
Check ____
Credit card: Visa ____   MasterCard ____
        Card number: _____
        Name on card: _____

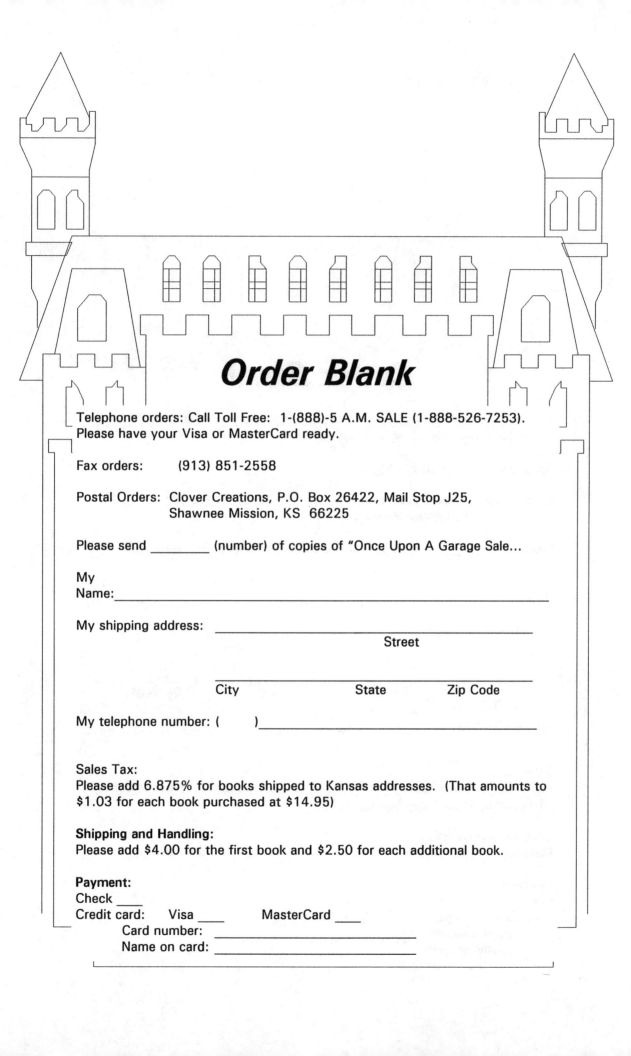

Order Blank

Telephone orders: Call Toll Free: 1-(888)-5 A.M. SALE (1-888-526-7253).
Please have your Visa or MasterCard ready.

Fax orders: (913) 851-2558

Postal Orders: Clover Creations, P.O. Box 26422, Mail Stop J25,
                Shawnee Mission, KS 66225

Please send _____ (number) of copies of "Once Upon A Garage Sale...

My
Name:_____

My shipping address: _____
                                     Street

                     _____
                     City   State   Zip Code

My telephone number: (   )_____

Sales Tax:
Please add 6.875% for books shipped to Kansas addresses. (That amounts to $1.03 for each book purchased at $14.95)

Shipping and Handling:
Please add $4.00 for the first book and $2.50 for each additional book.

Payment:
Check ____
Credit card: Visa ____   MasterCard ____
          Card number: _____
          Name on card: _____

Order Blank

Telephone orders: Call Toll Free: 1-(888)-5 A.M. SALE (1-888-526-7253).
Please have your Visa or MasterCard ready.

Fax orders: (913) 851-2558

Postal Orders: Clover Creations, P.O. Box 26422, Mail Stop J25,
                Shawnee Mission, KS 66225

Please send _____ (number) of copies of "Once Upon A Garage Sale...

My
Name:_____

My shipping address: _____
                                                    Street

                      _____
                      City   State   Zip Code

My telephone number: (   )_____

Sales Tax:
Please add 6.875% for books shipped to Kansas addresses. (That amounts to
$1.03 for each book purchased at $14.95)

Shipping and Handling:
Please add $4.00 for the first book and $2.50 for each additional book.

Payment:
Check ____
Credit card: Visa ____   MasterCard ____
          Card number: _____
          Name on card: _____

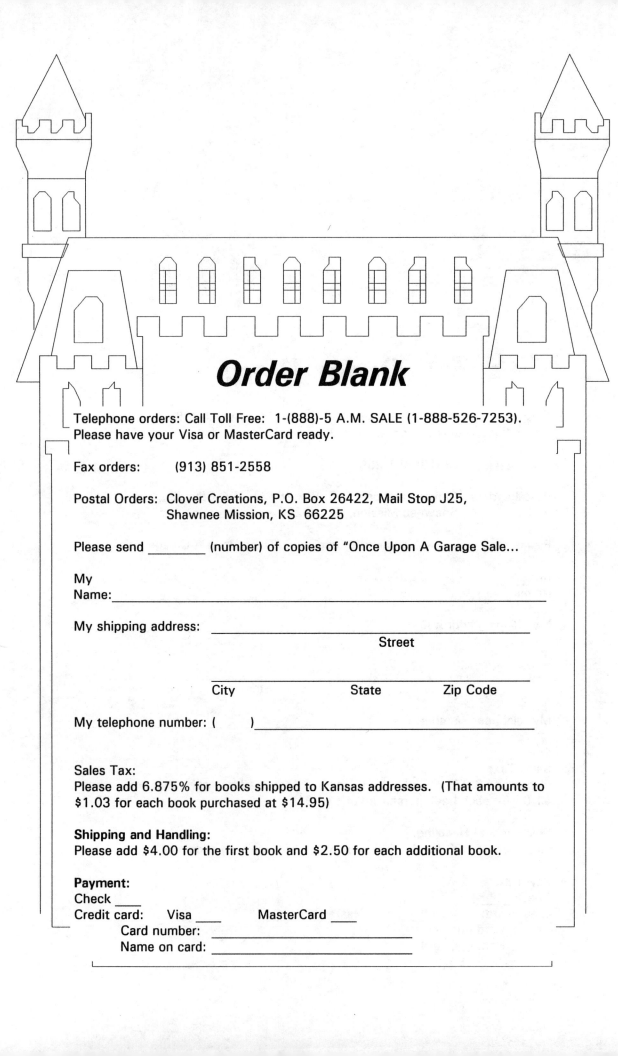